JOHN HOLLENBACH

with Pam Cressman

Through
the
Eyes
of the
General

Advantage
INSPIRATIONAL

To Kelly, Kris, and David, our children, and Tommy, Luke, and Abby, our grandchildren, your Mother and Nanny and I dedicate our lives, as told in this book by Patton, to each of you with our love.

Carol,

Thank you so much for your support for Joni & Friends

Blessings

John Hallenbeck

When Jesus spoke again to the people, he said, "I am the light of the world. Whoever follows me will never walk in darkness, but will have the light of life." John 8:12

When he was a boy, along with his brothers, he slept in the attic of their house. Because he, the last born of the family, was so much younger than they were, he had to go to bed long before the older boys. Nearly every evening he would have to go up the stairs alone, and for him that attic at night was a scary place. Who knew what lurked in the dark corners? What could it be that waited in the cubbyhole, that low closet where things were stored in the eaves under the back roof; what dangerous and alien beast might be waiting in there? Every night he'd turn on the light at the bottom of the steps and run to the top and across to his bed, not knowing what he might encounter.

But the family rule was that the overhead light had to be turned off; and the upstairs light switch was far across on the other side of that large, looming room. The challenge for him was to turn off that switch, get back to the bed, and hide in the covers before any of the mysterious and unknown night creatures could leap out of the darkness. Being pretty small, as hard as he tried he was never quite fast enough to reach the safety of his bed while there was still light. But his fear made him determined, and each night he raced across the room hoping to be out of harm's way before the dark descended into that frightening room. The memory of those nights and his childhood fear of the darkness stayed with him. And, once that boy became a man, he thought back to those early and very real fears alongside the truth that he would spend all of his days, as well as the nights, within the darkness of his blindness.

Chapter One

And now these three remain: faith, hope and love. But the greatest of these is love. I Corinthians 13:13

Before we get started, there are a couple of things I think I should explain. The first is that although some people call me The General, it's not my name. My name is Patton; but because my name is Patton, a lot of people call me The General, which is fine with me. I don't know very much about that first Patton, but I've heard it said he was a very commanding and important American military figure during the Second World War. Being named after a war hero, especially one with the rank of general is something I feel good about. The second thing is that I think it's best if I tell you right off that I'm a dog; and though I hope I don't seem boastful, I'm considered pretty unique because I've been trained to be a Seeing Eye dog.

But then I don't want to mislead you; this story is not just about me, Patton, nor is it only about my friend who happens to be blind. This tale is more than that, for it tells the story of the life of an individual who has had to learn to place all of his trust in a creature, a dog. We are designed to be assistants and companions to human beings in many different ways; as a Seeing Eye dog, I was specifically trained to work as a unit with a blind person. I was taught to get my master where he needs to be and to do it safely and with dignity while hopefully attracting very little attention to myself. My partner has also been trained to trust me to do those things for him. Of equal importance, you need to understand that the trust that he places in me is a mutual one, for I trust him the same as he does me. So I guess you could say that Through the Eyes of The General is our story, a tale of Patton and his master and the trust and love we have for each other. But then, as important as our relationship is, even that is only one small part of the story.

Because my good buddy and I are always together, we have learned to know each other very well. I've been with him while he's with his family, at his work, with his friends, and even on his different trips. Yes, we are nearly always together; and I've heard all his stories. Actually, I know them so well that sometimes it seems as if I know him completely even from the time before we were together. One important thing I've learned is that he wasn't always blind; many of his adventures took place, long before I knew him, when he could see just like most humans do. But before we jump ahead too far and get to all of that, it's probably a good idea for you to know a little more about me and how I eventually came to be a part of my good friend's life.

As I've said, my name is Patton; I got that name when I was born at The Seeing Eye in Morristown, New Jersey. I was named along with the rest of my litter of German Shepherd puppies, and all of our names started with the letter "P." Identifying litters with all the names having the same first letter is how The Seeing Eye keeps track of the many puppies that are born there and ultimately raised and trained to guide visually impaired individuals in their daily lives. Not all of the puppies born at the Seeing Eye are German Shepherds though people often think of my breed as guide dogs. They also raise and train Labrador and Golden Retrievers, a crossbreed between Golden Retrievers and yellow labs; and in some cases, when people have asthmatic conditions, they may use Boxers. For the most part, we are all bred and born at The Seeing Eye. But that's just the beginning. Having our litter taken care of as small puppies by the good folks there is just the start of our lives in the incredible world of human beings.

One day, when I was only eight weeks old, I was taken from my mother and siblings. This second beginning for me began when the good folks who took care of my litter at The Seeing Eye reached into our crate and took each of us puppies and gave us to different families. We sure didn't know what was going on, but much later I figured out that we were being introduced to the broader world of living with people. In my case, I went home with a wonderful couple that lived in New Jersey on a farm. Those nice people raised me for more than a year.

After getting over being separated from my mom and littermates, I was happy with the kind people on the farm. I would go everywhere with them; and they would feed me, care for me, groom me, and take me out on a leash. They were the first people to teach me how to behave. We'd go through different kinds of obedience exercises where they taught me those first things like learning to sit and stay. At the beginning, I wasn't too sure about the obedience thing; but after awhile it kind of got to be fun; you know, like a game.

Sometimes during the day I would go with the man to different meetings, and he would have me lie under the table. At first those times would seem too long, and I was a little rootchie. But after awhile I realized, hey, what's so bad? I could catch a few zzzzzs and kind of just chill. They would also take me to interesting places like restaurants and their grandchildren's baseball and soccer games. At home they had another dog who was kind of fun to be around. The lady of the couple was just wonderful to me; she gave me lots of hugs and took me for walks. It was a very good life. But just about the time I was completely used to everything we did together and thought that it was all fun, they took me back to The Seeing Eye. And they left me there.

That was the time I think of as my third beginning: for suddenly I found myself back at The Seeing Eye, and I have to tell you it was kind of strange. There are these people there they call veterinarians who poked and prodded and drew my blood and checked my hips; and well, I can't even describe everything they did to me, but basically it wasn't the best time in my life. Other than being lonely for my people, that is the first thing I remember when I think about my return. I now understand that the staff at The Seeing Eye needed to determine whether or not I was physically fit to become a guide dog. Because it is hoped that we'll be able to give long and healthy service to our masters, they make sure that we are in the best possible physical shape and that we don't show any weaknesses that might cause problems later.

After they finally finished examining me, the vets there, well they "fixed" me, if you know what I mean, so I wouldn't be distracted by other dogs when I was placed into training. Though I didn't like all the doctoring, I did like the kennel staff; they were fun and they helped me to stop feeling bad about leaving my farm family. The staff would feed us and put us out to play, and they had great toys for us. There were other dogs there, and it was all kind of nice. I even got to see some of my brothers and sisters again, and of course we made new friends.

Then one day there were about ten of us that were introduced to someone called a trainer. At first we just had a good time playing and getting to know one another, but soon it was time to get down to work. I've got to be honest with you; it wasn't all just play from then on. At least five days a week we were trained and disciplined to do lots of different things. I ended up liking my trainer a lot, but there were moments he had to be pretty hard on us. It was his job to teach us how to be obedient and how to work in harness and how that was different from a regular leash which is attached to our collar.

I soon learned that guide dog harnesses are made up of sturdy straps of leather that go around our shoulders and backs and attach under our chests; at the top there is a handle that is made of leather wrapped around steel. When we're working, the handle is our connection to the person we're walking with. In addition to learning the all-important communication through our harness, we also had to learn how to operate in traffic, how to behave and stay quiet in meetings, and generally how to be acceptable, as well as helpful, in a people world. On our walks our trainer talked to us a whole lot. One day he sounded especially serious after I had stopped on the street for just a little sniff at a pole, and he had to correct me.

"Now Patton," he told me, "all of this training is necessary, for you are going to have a very important job. You have to know how to help an individual who needs you because he can't see. You have to learn how to be his eyes. You will be leading the way through many dangers and barriers, and you need to know how to behave because you will be going into all the social settings of the people world. You must be serious about your work, so you can learn all you need to know to help your partner as you two negotiate your surroundings together."

I thought about what he was telling me. To be honest, I wasn't too sure what he meant; but I could tell by his tone of voice that I should try to follow all of his instructions. This pretty intense training process went on for about four months. From what I've heard, usually about five or six out of a group of ten learn all we must know to become a part of a person's need for assistance. Yeah, I admit that sometimes at the beginning I, too, resisted the discipline. I didn't like being put in harness before going out for walks; that part was pretty hard at first. I especially didn't like being taken out near all kinds of traffic with all those noisy cars and trucks. Well to be truthful, at first I just wanted to be back at the kennel playing in the yard and having fun with the kennel staff. But once I heard that not all of us learned enough to do the job, I didn't want to be one of the dogs that wasn't picked to help a person.

Every day my trainer would show up and the ten of us would go for a ride in a van; and then we'd go for walks with him in town, one at a time, so that we would learn how to look for cars that were turning into our path and how to stop and let those cars go by us safely. And we were taught lots of commands, such as "forward," "hop up," and "rest." Pretty soon I knew what all of the many commands meant, and I tried to do them as well as I could. We had to learn to stop at intersections, and to wait, and to be patient in meetings when the instructors would talk together. We also would go to restaurants where we had to behave and try to ignore sometimes very tempting food smells. We had to learn about disciplined park time, well you know, that's when you go out to relieve yourself. And we had to learn how to get into a routine, a routine of eating at 5:30 in the morning and going out to park and then going for runs, which were going into town and walking around while guiding our instructor.

Once we were well into training, I honestly thought that all ten dogs in our string, as the trainer called us, were going to make it. But then as we trained for first a month and then two months, a couple of the dogs were not with us anymore. I heard someone say that they had gone back to where they had been puppies with their families. In a way that sounded pretty nice to me; but I decided that was okay, I really did like my trainer and it got to feel good to do the things he wanted me to do. He praised me when I learned and remembered his training, and I liked that part a lot. This third new beginning in my short life did start out rough, but after awhile I realized the trainer was trying to discipline us in a way that made me believe we were going to do something very special. Even though I had liked it on the farm, I was feeling good that I was still being trained and not sent back there. I guess you could say that I was growing up.

Sometimes I think about that time when I was learning so much at The Seeing Eye. In fact, sometimes I even dream about it. You know how people will see a dog twitching while it's sleeping, and they'll guess that he's dreaming? Well, that is just what's happening, at least for me. In fact, last night I had a funny dream about one of my littermates. It went like this:

Ouch! Would you knock it off? OK, fine, you take the front of the wagon. I'll go in the back. It doesn't matter to me anyway. That Peyton, she can be such a brat. All eight of us are going round and round in our wagon, and it's so much fun. But that snippy Peyton always, always, always pushes the rest of us around so she can be the one in the front of the wagon. Well, I guess that's okay with me anyhow. I'll just move to the back and sit here and enjoy being pulled around the room and listening to the music. And every once and awhile there is a loud Bang! There's that noise that surprises us! I wonder why they keep having so much noise while we're playing this fun game; it sounds just like the streets when we're out on our training walks.

Yes, I remember so much of my time in training very well. I remember the good times we young dogs all had as well as the hard work; and I bet when I heard that bang again in my dream, I had a good leg twitch!

As our training continued, one day I heard one of the trainers talking to a woman who had on dark glasses and moved around slowly with a cane. He was describing a little about our training and then he told her that people also go to The Seeing Eye for their own kind of instruction. From what I understood of what he was saying, it seems that when they go to get their first dog, they remain there for four weeks of training and working with their new guide. If they are returning because their previous dog was too old to continue its work, they will stay at The Seeing Eye for three weeks.

He went on to talk more about how just as we dogs are trained, the visually impaired individuals must also be trained. Their stay at The Seeing Eye is a fulltime commitment; they don't leave to go to work or get to be with their families, and there are good reasons for this long stay. They must be taught the right commands and how to use the harness and the leash. They also need to learn when to correct us as well as when to follow us. They must work on how to cross at intersections where there is a traffic light and where there is not a light. They must be able to have good orientation to the world around them, and perhaps the most important thing is that they must develop a bond and trust with us, their dogs. As I've heard some of them say: Rule One is to trust your dog. Those four weeks are important for all those new skills to be learned. That woman seemed to be nice, but I never saw her after that day. Thinking back, I'm hoping that she did get a good dog to help her.

After we completed our training, we were taken out for our final work on the streets of Morristown, and the instructors actually let us guide them while they were blindfolded. On one particular day, our puppy raising families were invited back to observe the instructor in blindfold and the dogs that had been their pups working together on the streets of Morristown. I've heard that the families love doing this; at the same time, they must feel a lot of emotions. In their minds, they can still see that adorable, furry ball, their puppy. And now they feel such pride for having been part of the process of getting that little fluff ball to the point where it is a professional guide dog, ready to lead someone who cannot see, keeping him out of danger, and giving him dignity and independence.

I can only begin to imagine the emotion the puppy raisers must feel. I know that on the day they visited there were tears in their eyes. That was true for my family, that wonderful couple who had raised me. I recognized them right away, and seeing them there made me feel so proud about all that I had learned. At first I thought they might be taking me home with them, and in some ways that would have been fine with me. Yet at the same time, after those four months had gone by, I'd decided I enjoyed the routine in my new home. I liked being with the other dogs in my string, and I liked working with my trainer.

But then one day he took me over to what we called The Big House where there were all kinds of people. I had heard stories from our trainer about that house, and I was curious to see that both upstairs and downstairs there are a whole lot of bedrooms; in another wing there are spaces for dining rooms and lounges. It's a special place. As we walked through the different rooms, it all looked and especially smelled interesting; and I didn't know for sure, but it felt as if something was building up. I could feel it in my bones. Boy, they had really cleaned me up that day, taken me for a run, and made sure I went to park. I didn't know for sure, but it felt as if something different was happening that day, something big.

I remember thinking: Oh, we're now walking around in The Big House. Hmmmm, and now we're sitting in the lounge in the big house, my trainer and me. Then I started looking around, and I noticed a man coming toward us. It was interesting to me that he was using a cane, like the lady I had seen before, to get into the room. The next thing I knew he was sitting down across from me. I didn't think a whole lot about him, but I did notice that he wore dark glasses and that he was taller than most of the people in the room. My trainer was talking to him and calling him John; at first I couldn't understand everything he was saying, but then I heard my name.

"Patton is a fine dog. He's worked extremely hard. And he is a beautiful animal. His temperament is very mellow, very even. We chose him because he's a good size match for you, and I think you two will make a great team in other ways as well," he said.

Oh gosh, the next thing I knew my friend, the trainer, was taking me over to this stranger, and the man with a cane was putting a leash on me.

What was this? What was this tall man with the dark glasses doing putting a leash on me? He looked nice enough, but I didn't know him. And what was he doing with my leash, the one I wore when I was with my trainer? Oh boy I was feeling a little nervous, but he began petting me on my head. That part was okay, I thought; I always did like being petted.

Next, he was calling me by my name, and he leaned down and gave me a hug. I decided that wasn't too bad either and I would give it a little time. Then this man stood up, still holding my leash, and directed me out into the hallway; when I looked back, I couldn't believe that my trainer wasn't coming with us. We went into one of the rooms; and I have to tell you, this started feeling different. But I sniffed around a little bit, and it was actually kind of nice. There was a bed and a closet in the room and a door that went into a little bathroom.

Just as I was getting a good idea of the place, there he was kneeling down right beside me. I guessed he wanted to talk to me a little bit. As I said, he seemed kind enough, but, well I wasn't so sure. It was at that point I started to seriously worry: Where was my trainer? As I was becoming more concerned, this tall man with a nice smell, but one I didn't know, was petting me and sitting down on the floor with me. I decided that the best thing was not to look at him and just be patient. My trainer was going to come soon; I knew that. He was going to come very soon; and actually, I was starting to feel a little hungry. They hadn't fed me much that day. But even though I was hungry, this guy kept petting me.

He kept talking to me, too, "Yes Patton, I can tell that you are a beautiful dog. You feel so sturdy and strong, and your coat is just wonderful. I think we're both lucky to have been chosen for each other."

Oh gosh, I didn't know who this guy was, but he was getting just a little too lovey for me. Well, but then I thought, maybe not. At least he knew how to pet a dog in a nice way. And anyway, it didn't really matter because I knew my trainer would be coming to get me soon.

So now you have a little of my background and how I've come to tell this story through my eyes, The Eyes of the General. For you see, my trainer didn't come back for me that day and not the next nor the one after that. This tall man, the one I first saw walking with a cane, had come to The Seeing Eye for his new dog; and I, Patton, was to be that dog. After all my time and all my new beginnings as a puppy in a litter, as a growing puppy with the kind people on the farm, and as a young dog in training, I was prepared to be a full-fledged Seeing Eye Dog. And now I had my master, the person that I would be guiding, the man who, though I didn't know it that first day, was to become my best friend.

Chapter Two

You, O Lord, keep my lamp burning; and my God turns my darkness into light. Psalm 18:28

Yes, those are my memories of how I came to be a Seeing Eye dog; but I was soon to find out that it wasn't the end of new beginnings for me. I stayed with the man that I had come to know as my friend and partner at The Seeing Eye, and we trained together as he and I worked through all the commands that I already knew. He fed me, petted me, and played with me. We shared the same room in The Big House, and I didn't go back to the kennels even at night. I felt pretty comfortable after about three weeks with him, and I worked hard to do my job well. I did make some mistakes, and he had to correct me. But he also always forgave me right away for those mistakes and gave me lots of praise when I did what I was supposed to do.

We were learning how to be together as a team, and it was almost all good. I was still at The Seeing Eye, and by then I knew my way around pretty well. Yes, I decided, this working in a place I knew was going to be just fine. But then one day we left The Seeing Eye. We went home to my master's house and to his wife and family where I found that I had yet another new beginning to experience. I had new routes to learn and new places to go; and I'm proud to say, this time I felt ready for whatever path was ahead for me.

I soon learned that I was going to be living my life completely in a people world where I would get to know quite a lot about them. What I've found most interesting is that there is a parallel in their lives with mine. In each of my new beginnings, I learned to love and I eventually learned to lead with that love. What I grew to know is that my friend has learned and continues to learn those very same things in his own life. Since that first day that I met him at The Seeing Eye, we have spent nearly all of our time together. We have had many quiet times when we're alone taking our long and beautiful walks. Almost as often we've been with other people, usually his family and friends; and I hear all of them talk. It's pretty amazing how much you get to know about people by just listening.

Because of my training, I know to lie quietly when I'm working and people probably think I'm asleep; but over time, I've heard my friend, in many different conversations, talk about his life and experiences. One place we go a lot is right in our neighborhood. It's a small café that has a very friendly feeling. You go down a couple of steps from the street to get to the door. Once inside, there's a counter on the right with high stools around it. To the left there are a lot of tables with regular chairs, and that's where we always go. It's warm in the cafe in the winter, and it's nice and cool when it's hot outside. It smells so good in there because the kitchen is right behind the counter, and they are always cooking things that honestly make my mouth water. For my friend, though, I think the best part of going there is talking and sharing stories with people.

On Tuesdays we meet the pastor at our café, and on Wednesdays our good friend Chuck is there. Then on Saturdays his wife joins us, and we get to be with my master's sister and brother-in-law. Those are our regular trips. Sometimes we also join a bunch of guys who are just known as The Group. A few of them are still working at least on a part-time basis. The rest, though, are retired now like my friend. Basically these guys just sit together around a table at the café, drink lots of coffee, and solve all the problems of the world from politics to religion to events in our hometown. Well, you name it, they talk about it.

We're at that place so often I think maybe they'll put a statue of us outside, but I guess we shouldn't count on that. The waitresses there are always kind, and they guide us to the right place. As we go in, I'm always hoping to see someone I know. Sometimes when I do, it's hard for me not to want to run over and say, "Hello! I know you." One day last week we went in and my friend directed me to the left. We went to the table; and then he dropped the leash by accident, at least I think it was an accident. I saw a woman sitting at one of the tables who usually sings beside us in choir at our church. I ran over to her to say, "Hi, how are you?" I have to tell you she seemed absolutely delighted; and I could tell that, in at least a little way, I had made her day.

Through listening to all of his stories at the café and other places, I've gotten to know pretty much everything about my master, just the same way as very close friends do. So where did it all begin for him, what were his new beginnings? As I told you earlier, he wasn't always blind. He grew up believing himself to be a fully sighted child, and many of his experiences as a young man took place before he even began to know that he had a vision problem. In all that time, he thought of himself as having all the regular senses; and he probably just took that fact for granted the way most people do.

Other than his boyhood fear of the darkness and the challenge of going to bed in the scary nighttime attic, my friend always talks about having had a happy childhood. For almost all of his life, he has lived in the same small town, a fine place that has always suited him perfectly. From all that I've heard about it, I'd say that when he was a boy, it was as small town America as it gets; and in many ways it still is now. From what folks say, some things have changed, but in those days it was like something in a picture. Actually, believe it or not, around the time my friend was born, The Saturday Evening Post featured the town on the cover with a painting by Norman Rockwell.

Though only forty or so miles from a major city, it was, back then, a complete world of its own. Within just several blocks, you could get everything you needed whether it was groceries, clothes, or hardware; there were even two stores just to buy shoes. In that time, there were no malls and no shopping centers; there was no need to venture too far away from what you had at home. It was a town where you were related to many of the people; and if you weren't related, you knew them anyway. And they knew you. It was a safe place, a place where everyone watched out for each other.

My friend grew up in a large and active extended family. He lived with his parents, his two older brothers, his older sister, his mom's mother and his dad's father, all eight of them in that one house with just one bathroom. Their home was at the edge of town in the end of a row of big stone houses. It had a bay window that rose up on the side that looked out across an old brickyard. Downstairs there was a large living room with an old-fashioned eat-in kitchen at the back. On the second floor were three bedrooms and that one bathroom with a tub but no shower. The boys of the family all slept on the third level in that sometimes-frightening attic that served both as a sleeping and storage area.

Along with the boys' beds, there were chests and racks for the storage of the family's off-season clothes that often gave the room a distinct smell of mothballs. Linoleum pieces on the wood floor were the only real decoration. There was no heat in the attic in the winter, and in the summer the only air conditioning came in the breeze that flowed through the half screens that were fitted into the windows when the weather was warm. Though it all might sound a little humble by some standards now, it was a great house to grow up in. It was home, and it wasn't all that different from anyone else's in the town.

Actually, in those days, except for sleeping and eating, kids spent most of their time outdoors. One of the things that made my friend's childhood home special was the large open lot that the family owned next to the house. It was a perfect place for playing or having a catch. At the back of the yard there was a two and a half story barn with an upstairs equipped with a ping-pong table and other things that made it a great place to be on rainy days.

I always like to hear my buddy talk about his childhood home and family. I especially like a story I heard him tell his friends one morning at the café. The men had been talking about their town, and those who had lived there as boys were swapping stories about what life had been like in the old days. From what they were saying, it seems things have changed in some ways but in others have stayed about the same. Then my master began reminiscing about a very specific memory that had, for some reason, stayed with him across the years.

"I remember an early summer morning when I sat at the attic window looking out across the lot where we had our two gardens, a hedgerow, and many trees, including an apple tree and a cherry tree. I could see the first glimmer of light from the sun as it began to rise in the southeast. At first it was a slight yellow hue, and then I watched the peaking of the sun as it began to show over the tops of the trees at what we called the brickyard. Oh yes, some of you must remember the brickyard. For those of you that never saw it, it's where they used to make the bricks, a once thriving factory that produced most of the materials that were used in the early building of our town and the nearby villages. By the time we were boys, all the buildings were leveled with bricks lying all across a wide area.

"The site where they had dug the clay out for the making of the bricks was in those days used as a dump. Beyond that dump was a swampy area that led to a small plateau and then down to the Branch Creek. As the sky became brighter that morning, I could see about a mile up the stream where the concrete bridge had just been built to replace the old wooden covered bridge that had been moved to the nearby park; and it, too, was just becoming visible in the first light of day.

"As the sun lit the lot beside our home, I looked down at the garden in our yard. There were several rows of corn, peas, string beans, lima beans, and tomatoes, all rising out of the ground, fighting for space with the weeds that I, unfortunately, would have to pull. Those vegetables would be cooked and served almost straight from the garden for our evening meals or canned for the winter. The rows ran the full distance of the hedgerow that separated the back and front yards of the open lot. The front yard ran to the corner and there were several trees of varying types growing there; most of them were very nice for climbing with platforms built among the branches. In the back yard was another small garden where other vegetables such as onions and peppers were growing. This lot was about five feet lower than the rest of the property that the house was on and sat below the old barn at the back of our property.

"The light got brighter, and behind me I could hear the rustling of my brothers, who would soon be rising to go get breakfast and then head off to their jobs. One of them was a carpenter, and the other was working in the local glass factory where our father also worked in the office; actually, my mother worked there, too, in the shipping department. As far as I was concerned, that working was fine for my brothers because that got them out of doing the chores around our place. I, on the other hand, would have to make sure, as the sun got hotter, that the weeds were pulled, the grass was mowed, the sidewalks trimmed, the porch washed, and the steps swept. Oh well, the important thing was to get as much done as I could early, so I could play wiffle ball before lunch and get to the playground to play the daily double header with all the Playground Rats, as we called ourselves. As I was thinking about my day, I heard my mom's voice coming up the stairs.

"'Don't forget to mow the lawn and weed the garden,' she called up to me. 'There's cereal in the cabinet and milk in the fridge. Make sure you put the milk back in the fridge.'"

"'Okay, Mom,' I yelled back.

"Everybody was going off. I, though, would sit and let my mind wander for a little bit more, just kind of taking in the whole scene. All of them went to work; even my sister worked at French's, which was a place that made mustard. That's all I knew about what she did. Grandpop was at home with me, but he was usually out in the barn tinkering with the car. He owned our only family car; later on when Grandpop had to stop driving, my dad bought that car from him. It was an old '53 Plymouth; though I didn't know it at that time, later on when Dad got a new car, that Plymouth would be the car that I would drive in high school. Ah, but that's moving ahead.

"That summer morning, as I looked down over the field, I slipped into a daydream of being at the plate with the bases loaded; there were two outs and a full count. Now, here comes the pitch. Whack! A long drive to left center field, and that ball is out of here. A grand slam homerun! Wow! If only it was like that in real life. I bet just like you guys, I always imagined being the hero. Ah well. But then I was brought back to reality when I heard another instruction from downstairs.

"'Don't forget to do the dishes, as well.'

"'Okay, Mom.'

"Then, Bang! I heard the outside door closing as I tried to shake myself from my fantasy world and looked down again at the reality of weeds in the garden. Oh well, I decided, I guess I better get down there and start with the dishes."

All the guys laughed at this story before they starting chiming in with their own memories of being kids. They, too, remembered the way they spent their summer days with chores and baseball. One of them remarked about how long and good a day had seemed then, and they all agreed. Not one could recall a time when they were bored or needed to be entertained. In their memories, every day had been an adventure that they made for themselves; and most of the time the chores got done as well.

As busy as everyone in my friend's family was, theirs was one that always made time to practice its faith. They all went to their nearby church both regularly and often. His mother was a piano player, and they often stood around her as she played, singing the old hymns, especially at Christmastime. Through his family, he learned the unquestioned belief in Christianity that has sustained him throughout his life. He was also encouraged to learn more about his faith both at home and at church.

He grew with these important lessons along with his siblings who were all several years older than he was, and he always felt that having his two grandparents from either side of the family in his home was both a privilege and a blessing. Dinnertime among this large group was an especially important part of the day, with his brothers and sister arriving home from their work and activities and his parents coming home from their jobs in the local factory. Everyone had stories of the day to share with each other, and they always practiced evening devotions together.

But even good boys raised in traditional families seem to need to raise a little mischief, and my friend apparently was no exception. When it came time to start school, he decided it just wasn't for him. Actually, in first grade he worked out a great plan to avoid what he felt was a kind of imprisonment. One morning, after his father had walked him most of the way to the neighborhood elementary building, that clever boy decided he could sneak back home through the alleys. His idea was to hide and play in the barn until it would be time to come home from school. The scheme actually worked well for two days, and he enjoyed the freedom that he figured he had been pretty sharp to work out. The third day he waited for his dad to disappear over the rise in the street that would take him to his work. Again the reluctant scholar used this opportunity to change routes and run home. As he headed there, he was looking forward to all the great things he could do that day. Then he got back to the barn and opened the door to his refuge.

And there, inside the barn, stood his father. Fortunately, he was a man who rarely showed anger; but by the time he had walked his son all the way back to his school, the youngster came to realize that his precious moments of freedom were over. Knowing that his escape from school learning had come to an end, he comforted himself with the memories of those two days of adventure. From then on he resigned himself to attending school on a regular basis.

Another escapade that took place when he was young was brought on by his fascination with his oldest brother's taking up smoking. Sometimes his brother would send him up to one of the corner grocery stores which was a couple of blocks away from their house to get him a pack of Lucky Strikes and a pint of freshly dipped ice cream. The errand boy's payment for making the run was a double dipped ice cream cone for himself. The appeal of that smoking eventually led to the boy's sneaking a cigarette or two from his brother's packs. In the beginning he was pretty smart and only took one at a time, which he would then take to the barn to experiment with this forbidden vice.

On one of these little excursions to the barn, my friend decided that he needed to know how long a match could burn while in flight. And you guessed it: he accidentally set the barn on fire. This experiment gone awry resulted in a punishment by grounding that lasted for several weeks. That ordeal finally cured him of experimenting with the flight of flame and the effects of oxygen.

Fortunately, no one had been injured and the poor barn's worst damage was a scorched wall.

But he was still filching those cigarettes. Then he became a little greedier and one led to two and then more until his brother finally realized what was going on and set up a trap. Once the discovery was made, they had a serious discussion that involved his older brother's explanation of the evils of smoking, followed by the more ominous threat that he would tell their mom and dad if the devious practice continued. That conversation finally convinced the boy of the error of his ways.

Fortunately, most of the youngster's energy was soon absorbed in athletics. His whole family was very involved in sports, especially his brothers and their father; and they all played all the sports that were available in small towns in those days. I've often heard him say how very grateful he is that, although the eye condition that caused his blindness was probably affecting his peripheral vision even at a young age, the advancement of the deterioration of his retinas progressed slowly and in a way that neither he nor anyone else knew that he had a vision problem. As a child, he never knew that other people didn't see the same way as he did. He learned to accommodate with the vision that he had to compete in football, basketball, and especially baseball. And from what I've heard him say, he did love to compete.

He played Little League baseball, all the youth basketball leagues, and then played junior high football. By the time he was in high school, he had decided that he would play basketball to get in shape for baseball and that sport would be his real focus. Baseball was his father's first love and that was translated to all of his boys. Along the way, my friend kept growing taller. By the time he was in tenth grade, he was six foot three; but he didn't weigh a whole lot, probably not much more a hundred and sixty or sixty five pounds, even after a big family dinner. But the one thing that he could do was throw a ball very fast and very hard with some difficult-to-hit movement on it. As a freshman in high school, he played junior varsity baseball and actually pitched two exciting no-hitters for his team.

The following year he was invited to join the varsity, and they had a very good team. They were young, but they had two seniors who were the stalwarts of the club; one of them went on to be all state in both baseball and football and later played football at Duke and then coached at the University of Minnesota. Those two seniors were the number one and number two pitchers for their team. My friend, still only in tenth grade, was to be the number three pitcher.

Somewhere early in the season, the coaches decided to try him out and pitch him against one of the teams that was struggling in the league; that game was his first start in varsity baseball. To him, it was big stuff. Well, that day, as he tells it, turned out to be real big stuff, for at his first varsity start he had the wonderful privilege and opportunity to pitch a no-hitter. Now that might sound pretty spectacular, but if you look at the statistics you might wonder if for the most part the opposing batters were frightened and unable to hit because he struck out ten, walked seven, and hit three of them with the ball.

Then he tells the story of that spring day in his last year of high school. It was the final game of the year. His high school, which had won maybe four games out of a season of sixteen games, was playing the team that had just locked up the league championship. That day they sent their number one pitcher to the mound who was already at seven wins and no losses for the season. He was incredible, almost unhittable. And it was in this game that my friend got his last varsity start. It was a beautiful day, a warm spring day, which can be unusual for high school baseball season in our part of the country. Sometimes it can even be cold enough for there to be snow flurries. But that day was a beautiful one, and the home team set out to lock horns with the best team in the league.

They played seven inning games in high school; and after those hard fought seven innings, the score stood at 0 to 0. There he was walking out to the mound to begin the overtime eighth inning. The lead off batter lay down a bunt; my friend charged from the mound, picked up the ball and threw it. Unfortunately the ball flew over the six foot five first baseman's head into right field, and that runner made it to second. The next batter also lay down a bunt, and my friend proceeded to field the ball, turned, and made the play at first even though it moved the first batter to third; he then threw that ball into right field. By the time the inning was over, because of sloppy play and the loss of concentration, the local boys were down three runs. And they lost the game. Yet my buddy remembers that game as one of the most important that he pitched because his team was able to compete with the best in the league. That story tells me how much he loves the game.

When he thinks back on his athletic experiences now, he wonders how much his eye condition was already having an impact on his vision as a teenager. Looking back, he remembers times in practices and games when his basketball coach would yell at him, "You've got to see the whole floor." And he didn't quite understand because he thought that he did see the whole floor. But maybe he didn't. Having limits to peripheral vision can be a real hindrance to playing basketball. Or he thinks about playing baseball and pitching and how he would, with a man on first base, go into a stretch and have difficulty being able to pick up the runner and what kind of lead they had off of first base. At one point he even worked out a signal with his third baseman, who would let him know when to throw over to first to keep the runner closer. At the time, he blamed his nearsightedness on the problem and had no idea that it was something that would have a much greater impact on his life than just the need to wear glasses. In spite of the adjustments he sometimes needed to make, I have heard him say many times that he's always felt that he was privileged to be able to compete even though he had a condition that would ultimately cause him to go blind. But he didn't know what was ahead when he was growing up, and he thanks God that he didn't. Just think how different his life would have been if they, his coaches, parents, teachers, and doctor, had realized that his vision was slowly deteriorating from the peripheral to the center. They may well have kept him from playing baseball and basketball and doing all the things that so many boys like to do.

Chapter Three

And this is love: that we walk in obedience to his commands. As you heard from the beginning, his command is that you walk in love.   II John 1:6

Being involved in sports was certainly a big part of my friend's childhood, but that wasn't all that occupied his time and helped shape the man he was to become. As I mentioned earlier, church was a big part of his boyhood; and it was also where he found his closest friendships. There were five boys in their group, and they all went to the same church and all participated in sports in high school. Two of them were in the class ahead of my friend, one was in his class, and his best friend was a fellow in the class behind him. This boy also happened to be the six foot five inch first baseman that my buddy couldn't hit with a baseball.

These five were close as teenagers and have remained close into adulthood. As boys, all of them were in the same Sunday school class; and they often sat together during church services. In fact, two of them, along with my friend, received their God and Country award for their work in the church while they were teenagers as a part of Boy Scouts.

I've often heard him talk a lot about his best friend, Denny. Though he was in the class behind him, he was only six months younger. When he was small, my friend's mother babysat for him while his own mom went back to work; so the two boys were practically raised together and remained the closest of friends. They were so close that they were in each other's weddings. Denny was always highly spiritual, and he was always close to God. The two boys would meet in the morning under the staircase to the garage and have a quiet time of Scripture reading and prayer before they would go to school. It's obvious to me that their relationship with each other and perhaps more importantly their shared relationship with their

Master have held them together, even though they've been separated by many miles and by the differences in their careers paths.

Now, these two might sound too be to good to be true, but, from what I've heard, they could get into mischief as well. This story took place one summer day when the boys were around ten.

"Oh, Denny," my young buddy called to his friend. "Let's go. We've gotta go play wiffle ball. Everybody else is already down at the Arch Street School."

"I've got to quick mow the lawn," Denny answered coming around the house.

His lawn wasn't big; it was just a small front yard. If they worked together on the trimming and the mowing, they decided they could be done in fifteen or even fewer minutes.

"John, come on over here. There's no gasoline in the mower, and I'm not sure which of these cans is the gas."

"This one smells like gasoline to me," his helpful friend suggested.

"Okay, let's put it in," Denny said.

"Now it's got gas, let's get moving."

After pulling and pulling, "Now it won't start," was the frustrated Denny's response.

"What do you mean it won't start? Come on. Everybody else is already over there."

"No really, it won't turn over. Something must be wrong," Denny insisted.

"Well if it's not going to work; we're not going to get the lawn mowed, so let's go. We might as well go play wiffle ball."

So they left the lawn and the stubborn mower to meet up with the rest of the guys at the Arch Street School, which was only half a block away.

"You guys will be the Dodgers, and we'll be the Phillies," the boys agreed. In those days all the pro players stayed on the same teams, so they knew everybody's names and the boys identified with them. The bunch of Rats, as they called themselves, had a great time and finished their game, then the two best friends went back to

Denny's house before lunch. Feeling a little guilty, they tried to start the mower again, but it still wouldn't turn over. They finally gave up and decided that Denny's dad would take care of the problem when he got home.

The next morning when they met up at the playground, Denny told his friend guiltily, "Oh boy, is my dad upset."

In their rush to get to the game, the two had put kerosene in the mower.

So, as you can see, they weren't perfect. I like to imagine these two boys and their group of friends and all the good times and adventures they must have shared. I can especially imagine them day after day playing baseball under the summer sun; and when I imagine that fun, I realize I would have liked to have been with them. But in time, of course, as it must be with all golden boys, they all grew up and needed to make decisions about what they would do after high school.

Three of the group of five went on to college, while the other two, including my master, went to work in local factories after they graduated. Denny, who was an excellent athlete, had won ten varsity sports letters from his freshman to senior year in high school. He was such an excellent player that he went to a major university on a basketball scholarship. Interestingly, to underscore his spirituality, in time Denny gave up that scholarship to transfer to a smaller college in order to go into their divinity program. He later went on to seminary, and today he is a United Methodist minister.

I'm not sure when my good buddy realized there were girls, not just boys, in the world, and that they could be fun, too. But I do know from their stories that he began dating this one very special young girl named Judy when they were both seniors in high school. And I'm going to tell you a secret that even they didn't know at the time: that lovely girl was to become the most important person in my friend's life. Although they had been in the same class all through junior high and high school, they actually never met until they were seniors; and that's when the natural course of things drew them together. As it sometimes happens with teenagers, for a short time they parted and stopped dating; but happily for all of us, soon after graduation the two of them got back together. The attraction of young love would cause both of them to be seriously smitten with each other, and fortunately that was enough to get them over that little bump in their path. Some might say it was just meant to be.

Once they had their school years behind them, the two young ones began looking toward their future. Judy got a good job at one of the local elementary schools as a secretary. My friend originally went to work in a print shop; however, as it turned out it was one of those experiences in which he and his immediate supervisor were like oil and water. This combination just did not work. So, after a brief stint in the print business, he left that job to go to work at the local glass factory where, as I mentioned, one of his older brothers worked and where their father was an officer of the company.

I've often heard him say that such an arrangement, where your father is one of the big bosses, can make a difficult situation. Yet I also gather from my friend that he never actually saw his work there as his long-term career, even though he probably didn't realize that he was thinking that way at the time. The model of his brothers and most of his family from his father and uncles was to graduate from high school, get married, start a family, and work in one of the local businesses or industries. So that was the path he pursued.

It was during this transition period that an event took place that was probably the first step toward being adults in the maturity of these two young people. By virtue of being the youngest, my friend's older siblings all had already gotten married and had children. While the young couple was dating, they would often baby-sit for my master's nephews and nieces. As I mentioned, he worked with one of his brothers and this is the one who had two daughters and a son. These were the children that they babysat for the most, and they became very close to them. My buddy often talks about the times they spent with those three kids; he remembers how they played games and he bounced them on his stomach and chest as he lay on the couch. They were the first children that he learned how to take care of and to love.

On a cold Monday morning in January, my buddy went to work on what is known as a cutting crew where they shape the glass into what would become scientific slides. That crew was made up of his brother, two other fellows, and himself. But on this winter morning, he was surprised that his older brother didn't show up for work.

When he went home for lunch, he found out that his niece was sick. She was so sick that her parents had taken her to the hospital where the doctors determined that she had encephalitis. The prognosis was extremely grave, and the family was terribly worried all week. Sadly, on that Friday, the sweet little girl went home to be with the Lord. It is hard to imagine that a five-year-old girl, vibrant and lively, could in just one week leave this world. The grief and shock of the loss of this child deeply affected everyone who loved her.

For my friend and his soon-to-be wife, who were then eighteen and feeling in love with the whole world, the death of this little girl was a startling stopping point in their young lives. That night when they could finally be alone together, the young couple clung to each other as they tried to work through all of what they were feeling.

"I can't believe it. I just don't understand it," he said to Judy.

"I don't either. But God must have a reason," she answered.

"I know that's true. But she was so healthy, so beautiful, so full of life."

"Yes, she was. She was a wonderful little girl. I know how hard it will be for everyone to understand or even believe it's true for a while. And it will always hurt. I can't begin to imagine how your brother and his wife must feel," Judy answered.

"Helpless, angry. I know that I feel so helpless. And what can you say, what can you possibly say to your brother about this? What can you say to your sister-in law? It's just so hard, so impossible."

"I keep thinking about them, too, and my heart breaks for them. I think it's something that you probably never get over. Losing a child has to be the hardest thing that can happen to anyone. But you must just find a way learn to live with it. You have to. As horrible as this is, I'm so grateful they have their other two beautiful kids. They have to go on for them, and I think that's a good thing. I've heard older people say that time heals, and I hope that can happen for all of us," Judy said as she held tightly to his hand.

"But does time heal all things?" he asked. "I don't think it heals completely. But you have to put all this sorrow in its place. And you hold it there. Then somehow you find a way to trust that God has it all under control because that's what He has said. Living in this world it doesn't feel sometimes like He is in control. I keep thinking about all of this, and I start to think that I understand; but then, no I guess I don't. Except that I know I have to accept it because this isn't the first such terrible loss, even though it's our first. It sounds like I'm going in circles, and I guess I am. But I keep coming back to knowing that God is in control. That's what we have to hold on to."

Both my master and his wife often talk about that tragedy as being one of the most significant maturing points in their lives and how even their understanding and belief in God were briefly shaken. They remember how at first this death felt like a correction or punishment, but for what? What possible punishment could that innocent child have deserved? But they grew and soon came to understand that death, whether it comes at a young age or in old age, is part of the natural course of things in this world.

They came to know that this child's death had nothing to do with correction from God, but that it was part of the journey that each person must take. They were shaken, yet not to the point of walking away from their beliefs. As a matter of fact, if anything they came to grow and understand out of this loss that their faith could actually be stronger. Their first realization of their own mortality and the mortality of the ones they loved made them pause to wonder how people deal with the things of this world without a faith and belief in God.

The young couple, though deeply saddened, was matured by their loss; and they found strength through each other as well as through their faith. Sharing this experience and the comfort they gave to each other during this sad time also seemed to increase their feelings for each other. Theirs was no longer just a high school romance.

As it always must be for those who suffer a terrible loss, their day-to-day life went on. My friend continued to work at the factory and played baseball in a semi-pro league, while the love of his life worked in the elementary school. They saw each other almost every day and went on dates to the movies or bowling, or they would get together with their friends. As they continued to spend time together, they both grew to know how much they mattered to each other; and it wasn't too long until my good buddy asked the single most important question of the girl of his dreams.

"Would you like to spend the rest of your life with me?"

And she, thankfully, answered, "Yes."

From what I've heard, the most important decision and new beginning in the lives of people is to become married. I know that both my friend and his wife talk about their wedding and early-married life in this way. There they were, two teenagers standing at the altar in the beautiful church, making their pledge for life to each other. Did they, in all of the excitement of that November day, know what it would mean to each of them? Did they pay much attention to the words of the ceremony that night as their minds raced forward into being together and only seeing the wonderful possibilities? Perhaps they didn't even really hear the words: "For better, for worse, for richer, for poorer, in sickness and in health." But although they may not have been focusing on those vows at that moment, they have honored them and lived by them for more than forty years.

I can almost picture now how beautifully the church was decorated with all the flowers and the candles that were glowing as the bright day turned into the early winter evening. All their friends and family were there. As the groom stood proudly at the altar, the wedding party marched toward him. His bride's maids-of-honor came down the aisle first, dressed in their pretty blue dresses.

Then as the music swelled, Judy, the lovely woman who would be beside him all his life, slowly walked toward him with her father at her side. He could not begin to describe how beautiful she was dressed in her white velvet gown, her face only partly visible behind the filmy veil. Did he, just past boyhood himself, have any real idea of all that she would mean to him and he to her across their lives? How could they know what the next year, two years, ten, twenty, even forty years would bring? But then, what did they care about those distant times in the future? They would be together, and being together was what mattered most to them that day.

By the time the ceremony was completed and the vows exchanged, it was raining outside; and I've heard them say that they thought that was a symbol of good luck for their marriage. After their reception and refreshments, the newlyweds couldn't wait for all of the ceremonies to end, to say thank you and goodbye to their loved ones, so that they could get on the road. They were headed to Florida for their wedding trip, a full week for them to be alone with each other and begin their time as husband and wife.

Chapter Four

Let us not become weary in doing good, for at the proper time we will reap a harvest if we do not give up. Galatians 6:9

I've heard Judy say that their beautiful November wedding had originally been scheduled for February and that moving up the date for such an important event had required a great deal of effort. But even though the planning had to be sped up, everything had turned out to be just as they wanted. The reason for the date change was that my master had received notice from the United States armed forces that he had been drafted and that he had to report after the first of the year. There was a military draft in those days because things were heating up for the United States in a Southeast Asian country called Vietnam, and all young men along with the families and young women who loved them lived with the fears and uncertainties that they could be called up at any time.

In September, after receiving that dreaded letter, my friend went for his army physical and found out that he was fit enough to be drafted. On his way home that day, he stopped in at the selective service office and asked when he might expect to be called into the army. They informed him that it would take place not before Christmas of that year but very soon thereafter. Had they waited to celebrate their marriage on the February day they originally wanted, he would have possibly already been a part of the military. They had no idea what that could mean to them, and it seemed unlikely that they would have been able to go on the honeymoon trip they were so much anticipating. They sat down and discussed whether it was better to wait until later, after boot camp training; or should they move the wedding date up sooner than originally planned? Though it meant they would have to speed up all their arrangements, the decision was made to have the wedding earlier and the big day became November twenty-sixth. After their honeymoon, they returned home to await the next major transition in their lives.

Not long ago, I heard my friend reliving his first day serving his country. It was a cold January morning; and, as he tells it, he along with two of his friends from home, stood among fifty young men at the U.S. Army Induction Center in Philadelphia. None of them knew what was ahead for them, and they waited nervously until a formidable sergeant entered the room.

"All rise. Gentlemen," said the sharply dressed, imposing figure, "I am Sergeant Hamilton; and you are now a part, a very proud part, of The United States Army."

Then the fifty young men, under his direction, took the oath to defend the United States of America and, if necessary, to die in its service. Since they heard on the news that the United States had ramped up its troop commitment in South Vietnam to protect what was supposed to be democracy from communist takeover, they all knew they were just the latest crop of young men to be drafted to the call of our government's commitment.

After they took the oath, Sergeant Hamilton continued, "Please be seated, gentlemen. Now this morning, we need five volunteers for The United States Marines. They have been unable to meet their monthly quota, and we need five of you fifty young men to volunteer to serve in the U.S. Marines."

They all looked down to avoid the sergeant's intense gaze as it swept around the room, and there were no volunteers to go to the U.S. Marines that morning.

After that long, silent pause, Sergeant Hamilton went on as if he wasn't too surprised, "All right then. I will leave this room, and I'll pull five files. When I come back in here, I'll read off the names of the *volunteers*, and you'll come up and get your file and go through the door behind me to see the Marine Corps recruiter. And the five of you will say nothing. You had your chance to volunteer, and now we'll do the volunteering for you. Let's just say it's your first opportunity to participate in our fine military discipline."

Sergeant Hamilton left the room and when he returned told the anxious group, "Gentlemen, these are the men who will be proud members of The United States Marines...."

The third name he called was my friend's. He did as he had been instructed: he got up, walked through the door with his file, and found himself with four other reluctant volunteers, along with the true Marine inductees, all getting themselves ready to leave for a trip by plane and train to Charlestown, South Carolina. From there they were to go by bus on to Parris Island and the Marine Corps Recruit Depot. When my friend tells this story, he admits that if he had known on that day he had a serious eye condition that would have disqualified him from service, he certainly would have volunteered that information and avoided being part of the military draft. But, at that time, he didn't know.

In those days he was one skinny, teenaged boy, who had just gotten married and now had to leave everything behind to serve his country, to do his duty because he was, after all, one of the children of The Greatest Generation. He then goes on to say that, although he would have probably used that information about his vision to avoid the draft, today he is both glad and proud that he did serve as a United States Marine.

Even though the events of that day were very serious and more than a little bewildering, my friend does remember part of it with good humor. He was in a layover in Washington that afternoon and called his bride of two months and explained what had happened that morning and that he was on his way to Parris Island.

After a brief silence, Judy said, "You're going to Paris? You mean you're going to France?"

After a second's pause, he answered, "Well, no, this is not the Paris that's in France. This is Parris Island; it's a Marine Corps training facility on an island off the coast of South Carolina."

To this day they often laugh that they were so naïve that they didn't even know where Parris Island was or what it meant to be in the Marines. But they found out, and they also learned that it wasn't all that bad. They were fortunate enough to be stationed at Camp

Lejeune for his two years of service. He considers his assignment especially good fortune because the two friends that he went to the Army induction office with on that January day were not so lucky. Though they were inducted into the Army rather than the Marines, which seemed a good thing at the time, they were assigned to serve in Vietnam. While there, they like many soldiers were exposed to Agent Orange and both died prematurely of cancer.

I've heard my friend asked how he could do all that he needed to do in the Marines, with their legendary rigorous training when he had such a serious eye condition, one that was increasingly affecting his vision. That it hadn't been picked up in physicals and in training is a bit mysterious. But that it was affecting him was, looking back, becoming increasingly clear. He tells this story about his days in training.

"It was February, and it was a cold, gray morning to be standing on the rifle range. We trainees had just completed the off hand position firing on our targets and were moving back farther away from the targets to take the prone position. We were to hit the deck and then squeeze off ten rounds in succession on our targets as fast as we could. The drill instructor signaled us with a whistle; I hit the deck and fired.

"I felt good about the ten rounds I'd just squeezed off. I stood back up, standing at ease with my weapon at my side. Suddenly, there was a Maine Corp drill instructor in my right ear, yelling and screaming at me. He then looked down, pointing at my target and swearing a blue streak. I saw ten red flags, known as Maggie's drawers, flash across my target, one red flag for each round I had squeezed off that had missed the goal. Another drill instructor was telling the next guy that they couldn't give him a score because twenty rounds, not ten, had ended up in his target."

Fully intending to have done his best, my friend had fired on the target to the right of him, not his own. Though he certainly didn't know it then, this was probably another sign of how his vision was not what it should have been. It's strange to me that the Marines didn't notice the problem, or maybe they did and that was why he was never sent into combat.

It seems as if the Marines should have especially wondered on another day at boot camp when running the confidence course, he leapt to the top of the next barrier which was made up of logs nailed at an angle, from a height of about six feet down to one foot off the ground. They were to hoist themselves to the top above the logs and run down them to the ground and then proceed on to the next barrier in the course. On that day, as he was running down the logs, he didn't see the drill instructor standing on the one foot platform at the bottom with his hands on his hips yelling, "Move it, move it, move it."

When they collided, the sergeant went down backwards with his trainee landing on top of him. As you might imagine, what that drill instructor had to say isn't something that can be repeated. The amazing thing is that when running that course, they always took off their utility shirts and their hats, or covers, as the Marines called them. If they wore glasses, they left them in formation, too. So when the drill instructor asked my master, with all the politeness a Marine drill instructor can muster, to please get off him, he immediately pushed up and ran to the next barrier which was a rope swing across sand and then on to the rope climb and then back to the formation. Once there he quickly put on his utility shirt, his cover, and his glasses. That drill instructor never could figure out which one of those "blind" Marines had run him over.

There is another story from his Marine training that I believe foretold my friend's diminishing vision. During boot camp there was the day that the drill instructors tried to move him into the front line at the left end of the four abreast formations that they would both run and march in. They soon realized that he had the tendency to drift out away from the formation itself and decided that they couldn't have him in the front where it was their practice to march the taller Marines. And he was among the tallest. So was this tendency to drift away from the line one more indication of the loss of peripheral vision? It seems likely.

After boot camp, the new Marine spent four weeks in infantry training at Camp Geiger in North Carolina, which is a small training camp and rifle range near Camp Lejeune. From there he was sent to supply school where, after completing the required classes, he received orders and was assigned to his duty station at Headquarters Company, Supply Second Marine Regiment, Second Marine Division at Camp Lejeune. As soon as he was assigned, he rented a military housing trailer and called his wife to join him. That's when the two of them were catapulted into their married life together. They had lots of adjustments to make, from learning to be in the Marines to creating a new feeling of family, now that they were living so far away from their parents and brothers and sisters.

They set up housekeeping in a nineteen-foot long by eight-foot wide metal trailer in a military trailer park. Their first home together had a small sitting and eating area, a tiny kitchen, and an even more miniscule bathroom. Then there was their bedroom where the bed was tightly enclosed in three walls; they propped the bed up on cinder blocks to make a little extra room for storage.

Financially they were really pretty poor. Judy received a monthly allotment of ninety-five dollars and after the government took the trailer rent out, he took home a whopping forty-four dollars a month. But they survived. They survived on love, and they knew that it would be temporary. From their stories were things always perfect? Were they always harmonious? Let's just say it sounds from their stories as if they were learning the early lessons that all very young couples must. My friend will readily admit that he grew and matured a lot more than his new wife did in those early days; and he also acknowledges that, as is often the case with young men, it was because he had more growing to do.

So there they were, living in a trailer with hundreds of other Marines and their young families close by; those government-housing trailers stood together in long, tightly packed silver rows. None of those young people had much money. But even in their humble financial situation at the time, there was something called Navy relief; and the young people were able to obtain clothing and diapers and all kinds of good will help for little things from the Navy relief organization that was a part of the camp. Yet even with that appreciated help, money was always very tight. In fact, my master and Judy were one of the few couples who had a car; just paying the maintenance and gas on that car was a real challenge, while still making sure there was always food on the table. Fortunately, from the first, Judy had the amazing ability to make great meals on almost no money.

They made a lot of new friends; some, even after so many years, are still in contact. But for the most part it was difficult to make lasting relationships with other couples, especially at that time when the United States was committed to a twelve-month rotation of troops in Vietnam. Actually, for the Marines it was thirteen months, but my pal the former Marine, says there's an old joke that Marines can't count. But the truth was that most of the people they became friends with were rotated out within six months after they had gotten to know them.

As my friend looks back over his spiritual journey, he remembers that while both he and Judy had always expressed their faith and belief in Jesus Christ, it wasn't something they talked about often. Beyond saying prayers at meals or maybe having occasional prayers when they were concerned about something or each other or someone else they loved, they didn't practice any formal religious devotions. Unlike at home, they didn't attend church or any kind of a Bible study group. Yet those young Marine couples that they lived near interestingly seemed drawn to them because of their faith. Many of those couples were younger than my buddy and his wife. There they were, a mere twenty and twenty-one years old in their time at Camp Lejeune, and they seemed to some like the old timers.

It was not unusual for them to know couples in which the husband was eighteen or nineteen, and some of their wives were as young as fifteen or sixteen. Such was the time in the United States when many of the young men of America did not, at that point, go on to college or have some kind of job deferment. As in all wars, the fodder for the cannons was very young. As the "older couple," they found a lot of people coming to them for different reasons; the other even younger women asked questions of the learning-to-cook-herself wife about how to prepare food, even, believe it or not, how to heat a can of beans. Since they had a car, they also provided the transportation to go to the movies or shopping. In addition to these day-to-day matters, some of the other couples also asked them about their faith. There were four couples who were especially interested in learning about their beliefs; they seemed anxious to be with people who could help to provide the spiritual guidance they were seeking.

Because of having a car, my buddy also found himself on several occasions taking young wives to the hospital when it was time to have their babies. He loves to tell the story of one trip to the hospital when he took his neighbor in to deliver her child because her husband was on a Caribbean cruise with the Marines. When they got there and the soon-to-be mother was safely inside, the attendant helped her to sit in a wheelchair and started pushing it toward the elevator.

Then the nurse looked back and said, "Well, aren't you coming upstairs with the little mother?"

And he replied, "I would be glad to, but I'm not sure how her husband would feel about it."

He's often wondered what they thought at the hospital because, if they had taken any notice, they would have seen him there so often.

One thing he always adds when he talks about his time in the Marines is that he always found the officers to be sympathetically aware of the circumstances of those young, non-commissioned Marines who were married, especially those who had children. Though they still had to do their job, the treatment from almost every officer was nothing but kindness and respect within the framework of the military chain of command.

The other morning when my friend and I were at our local café, he and some of the other men that he talks with there were remembering stories from their times in the military. I had just moved around a bit under their feet, trying to find a more comfortable position, when I heard my buddy telling this particular incident that told a lot about him and his early days of being married and being a Marine.

"Unfortunately, he said, "I learned very quickly how to walk, act, and talk like a Marine; and that meant I had a tendency to swear and use certain words that, well quite honestly, I didn't use when I was growing up here in town. But those words were commonplace in the Marine Corps. This language really did bother Judy quite a bit. There was this one day and we had an argument, as young married couples sometimes do. I was using my Marine Corps language to emphasize the importance of what I had to say, and Judy became very upset and went out the door.

"She was determined to get into the car and drive to her parents' place which was then in Norfolk, Virginia, about a four hour drive away. This left me sitting in our nineteen-foot long trailer, contemplating what I was about to lose. I sat there regretting how I had been acting and thinking about the fact that I should be trying and striving to be more like Jesus, and instead I was almost on automatic pilot to be just like everyone else.

"In the midst of this, if you will prayerful mood, I looked over on the counter by the sink and saw the only set of car keys. This of course made me realize that she could not be driving too far. Within a few more minutes, I don't remember exactly how long it was, it might have been fifteen or twenty, Judy came back in to the trailer and walked over to me.

"She sat down at the table across from me, and I said, 'Dear, I am very sorry; and I would like to sit here and tell you that I'll never say those things again, I'll never talk like that again, especially to you; but I'm not sure that I can keep that promise. But I hope it's enough that you know that I love you and that I want to love you even more. I want to love you in the way that a husband should love his wife, the same way that Jesus loves the church.'

"That was an important moment in our lives, for we both realized, perhaps even more than on our wedding day, the meaning of those all-important words: For better, for worse, for richer for poorer, in sickness and in health."

Then he added, "Oh yes, both of us were perfect from that day forward, right? Ah well, I think you know that's not true. But it was one of the steps in the journey from which we both learned and grew and developed us into whatever we are today."

The other men laughed, a little ruefully, I thought. My guess is that all of them had similar memories of their early days as husbands and the lessons that they had all needed to learn. With that, the waitress arrived with more coffee all around; and I had finally found a comfortable position between my master and the heater on the wall. So I took a little doze, still aware of the quiet rumble of the men's voices and their easy comfortable laughter. While I was resting, I thought about the fact that people, including my buddy, can make mistakes, just like we dogs do. It sure is good they know how to forgive as well.

Chapter Five

And let us consider how we may spur one another on toward love and good deeds. Let us not give up meeting together, as some are in the habit of doing, but let us encourage one another-and all the more as you see the Day approaching.   Hebrews 10:24 and 25

So there they were, the newlyweds, all snug in that miniature military trailer of theirs at Camp Lejeune in a place called Camp Knox. It was there that they created their first home together; and though it was small, it wasn't to be too long until it would be time to make room for a very precious addition to their family of two. For by the time my master had finished boot camp, his bride had shared the wonderful news that they were expecting a baby. It was shortly after that time that she had been able to go to North Carolina to start her life together with her Marine husband.

The two young people, only married ten months, had both just turned twenty when the big day arrived. It was a Sunday, and fortunately my friend was home from his duties in the Marines. Suddenly, he heard Judy calling to him.

"John, my water broke!"

His first thought was, "What? Ah, this government housing, you just can't trust it."

But then he heard her excited answer, "No, not that water; the baby's coming."

As you can imagine, once he understood what was happening, he reacted very quickly. In fact, he was so eager for this moment that he darted out the door and headed for the car. And just as it happens in old comic strips, he almost forgot his wife in his hurry. But then he gathered his senses and his wife, and the two of them got into their car and headed the four miles to the U.S. Navy hospital on Camp Lejeune. As he thinks back to that day, he remembers that afternoon as a blur; and he thinks it must have been the same for Judy.

But they arrived safely at the hospital, and the attendants there took her upstairs to the maternity section. Then the soon-to-be-father wound up waiting. And waiting. He remembers that it seemed like forever though it really wasn't; for in a relatively short time for such events, their first child, their wonderful daughter Kelly was born. I've heard him say that the sense of excitement, fear and then great joy, which this event brought to Judy and him, is very hard to put into words. But there she was, their little baby Kelly, a part of God's miraculous creation; and they were awestruck that they had unbelievably participated in the miracle of creating a new life.

Along with all the wondrous feelings he was experiencing, my master suddenly had the earth-shaking realization that he was responsible for these two people, for this young woman and their child. To this day it's difficult for him to describe all of his emotions and complex feelings. But he does say that taking them home from the hospital was one of the truly momentous events in his life.

There was not a lot of room in that nineteen foot trailer, so he had set up the baby's crib by removing the legs on one end and securing it on top of the couch with the legs on the other end still attached and resting on the floor. It wasn't a perfect arrangement, but it worked well enough for them. They were later able to get a slightly larger trailer, and between the kitchen and living room area there was a hallway that led to the bedroom and bathroom. In that hallway there was a chest of drawers on one side and on the other there were bunk beds. The young dad took the crib apart and made a railing on the bottom bunk out of one side of the crib, so that they could have the baby sleep in the hallway instead of having to take up half the couch to have the crib set up there.

Looking back now, they both realize how naïve they had been and how fast they had to learn what it meant to take care of a new baby. In truth, having had older brothers and a sister who had children, his nieces and nephews, my friend had a little more exposure to babies and young children than his wife did. But then love overcomes even the fear of doing something wrong, and his wonderful bride soon proved herself to be a natural as a mother. Even

I can see how new babies seem so fragile and so totally dependent on their parents. To tell you the truth, babies kind of scare me because I'm so afraid that I could hurt them; and I guess that even people can have those same feelings.

Today my master and Judy remember well how much they sensed and felt that responsibility; and they also recall that, at the same time, they learned to live with a new sense of both purpose and hope. I think he has come to believe that becoming a parent is a little bit like coming to understand who Jesus Christ is, for then a new creation occurs spiritually. When people are first aware of Christ's saving grace, they, too, are like newborn children; and they are dependent on Him. My friend talks about how a believer grows spiritually, just as a baby grows; God through his son Jesus and other fellow believers teach the maturing of spiritual growth, just as parents have the privilege of teaching and guiding a young life to maturity and womanhood.

Before they could get their feet fully on the ground and come to a complete understanding of what it meant to be a mom and a dad to a baby, Judy learned that she was again pregnant and that they were soon going to have another child. I think it was good that they were so young and, well, kind of innocent and that they had no sense of what it takes financially to have two children when the sole breadwinner is a private and soon to become a lance corporal in the Marines.

Those promotions helped, but let's face it, financially it would not be a decision that anyone would make. Fortunately, their lives did not start from a point of planning economic success and purpose but from the point of trust and love. Although they didn't have much in the worldly sense, what they offered to each other and to their baby in their love and devotion were more important than the material things of this world.

So it was as the young couple, with one daughter to care for, headed into the second year of their tour of duty in the Marines. Soon after their twenty-first birthdays, they were making plans for the entrance of their second child. On a beautiful September day, one year and a little over two weeks after the birth of their first baby, they were blessed with the arrival of their second daughter, Kristine. As quickly and smoothly as the first birth had gone, this second one took two trips to the hospital. Beautiful little Kristine came in with a little more kicking and screaming than Kelly had. From the first, these two perfect beings displayed their own individuality; their parents were delighted that each child was special and unique and imprinted with her own distinctive talents and personality.

The babies' grandmother flew down to North Carolina to help them with the two children and to assist them in getting on the right footing when Judy and Kristine came home from the hospital. Her presence was a tremendous help. But, of course, they didn't have a lot of room, so mom didn't stay long. Soon they found themselves, a young couple with two children, starting to think about what was next. From what they say when they reminisce, they think that both of them had to mature very quickly from being inexperienced teenagers into first husband and wife and then mom and dad. What they were to learn was that their two baby girls would grow and change every day, and each of them could easily return the love they were offered. It was an incredible experience to watch and love their children's distinct and separate personalities emerging.

As the babies grew, my friend's tour of duty with the Marines was nearing its end. Though the Marine Corps encouraged him to ship over for three more years, he felt he had served his responsibility to his country; and since he wasn't interested in a career in the military, he began looking at his options in civilian life. One idea came in a letter from his dad who told him that he had talked to a friend who was looking for someone with military experience behind him who was willing to go into his business at the entry level; they would even send the new employee to school. My friend and Judy both thought this sounded like a good opportunity.

There was also a civil service job in Norfolk in the Navy film library that was a possibility they considered. After talking with his father's friend over the course of several months, my friend made the decision that they would return to their hometown and begin this new job; and he planned on taking them up on the offer of going to school while working.

In October, with his tour scheduled to end on January tenth of the next year, my master and Judy moved their two children and their few belongings back to their hometown into a two-bedroom apartment. Reassured that his wife would have the support of family members and friends, he returned to North Carolina to serve out his tour of duty; and this time he lived in the barracks as he had in boot camp. In many ways, he was quite a bit more mature when he returned to living with the other men than he had been when he was in boot camp almost two years before.

He was a seasoned Marine now; he knew the ropes. The time of living away from his boyhood home had also taught him a great deal; he was no longer the green small-town boy he had been. Most importantly, he had all of the experiences of learning how to be a husband and a father; he now knew both the joys and responsibilities of those very adult roles. Yes, in many ways he was a different young man from the boy who had traveled to Parris Island for his initial training.

With his broadened experiences, he noticed things after he returned to living with his fellow Marines that hadn't been so obvious to him before. One thing that struck him was the unfortunate separation of the races, the regrettable prejudice that existed between the black Marines and the white Marines. Though he didn't like what he saw, he realized it was reality. He had worked with and for black sergeants and had played sports with several of the black Marines in their barracks. Those shared experiences made him feel the same kinship with them as he did with the white Marines. His disappointment with the kind of treatment that happened between the races in the barracks made him think about his Bible training and the things that he had both learned and believed.

He thought especially of the passage in which Jesus was challenged by the Pharisees as to what is the greatest Commandment, and He responded, "The First Commandment, To love the Lord your

God with all your heart, and all your mind, and all your soul; and The Second is like unto it, To love your neighbor as yourself."

He knew that God gave us The Commandments that we might understand that our lives are to be led by love, first through acknowledging the love of God for us, and second by our returning that love by acknowledging who God is and by demonstrating that love by leading and helping others. In the Marines my master grew in his understanding of the fundamentals of his faith, and he believed that God sent Jesus to live with men on earth so that they could learn to love their neighbors as they loved themselves.

There was one particularly interesting incident that took place in the barracks that spoke to him about how God works in people's lives without their even realizing it sometimes. Not long ago, I heard my friend relating this story and I must say I thought it was interesting. One night he was tired and decided he was going to try to hit the sack early. He was on the top bunk in the barracks and was just settling in for the night even though the barracks were still noisy as was always the case until at least ten o'clock.

Suddenly, another Marine came over and said, "Hey, wake up. They tell me that you're a Christian."

Still half asleep, he said, "What? What are you talking about?"

"You heard me," the other fellow answered. "They told me you're a Christian."

He sat up in his bunk, completely surprised but waking up fast, and responded, "Well yes, I do believe in Christ. But, how did you know?"

The answer he got back was that the other guys had been talking about him.

My master was truly shocked that the belief that he held within him could possibly be seen by others. After all, just like the other guys, he was a Marine. He was a warrior with all that implied: he talked like one, he walked like one, and he was even arrogant like one. How could anybody know about his belief in Jesus Christ? Soon he jumped down out of his bunk and within a short time there was a group of about twelve Marines of both races arguing and challenging and cajoling each other about their religious convictions.

The conversation went round and round with questions of, "Why do you believe?" "What do you believe?" "And why don't you?" And loud answers of, "You gotta be kidding" and "Look, I saw this awful thing happen. And look how people act. How can there possibly be a God?"

Back and forth the arguments and fears and doubts went, and my friend would repeat what he knew to be the truth. He remembers that probably no one in that group ever went to sleep that night. As he told this story, my master added that he had no idea what influence his simple faith may have had on any one of them, but to this day he remains surprised how God can shine through even when we think we're being the toughest. For what could be tougher than a group of hardened Marines? But there they were, in the middle of the night, sharing their doubts as well as their beliefs, looking for answers to their most deep-rooted fears and hopes.

At one point he said to them, "Look, I know we can rely on God; I know that He can give us freedom. We no longer need to be a slave to sin. With Him we can have an independence with more dignity than we've ever sensed before."

Another of the group named Mike added, "Listen to him, guys. Each day I start by trying to be in prayer that God might be present in my life. But you know, when this journey is finished, it's not over. For when Christ came to earth he suffered and paid my debt and then he died on the cross for me. But it wasn't over there because three days later he rose from the dead, which gives me and can give to you, too, the wondrous hope and the promise that He will return one day for all of us and that we will all know the physical bodily resurrection that he proved. On that day whether it is sooner or later, we will no longer have to be afraid.

"That is indeed where I want to be, in His Heavenly Kingdom," Mike added. "And whatever time I have on this earth, I just hope that I can be a better person each day at the new beginning than I was yesterday. And I hope that I can be part of Kingdom building for Him.

I invite you, if you do not today know who Jesus Christ is, to consider the evidence for who he really is and invite him to enter His Light into the darkness of your heart, so that your fears might be removed and that you will no longer sense the destructive power of fear."

As my friend listened to the convictions of this fellow Marine, he wondered again how the others had known of his strong-held beliefs. He was still feeling amazed that he had been chosen to be part of the conversation. Then he remembered that in the Scriptures we see that personality and character always appear and that God uses these personalities to spread the truth of His word.

With that thought in mind, he said to the group, "There are so many examples of how God works in this world. Look how God used Captain John Newton, who had once been a slave ship captain, and how it was his influence that won over William Wilberforce to later cause the British government to put an end to the slave trade. You see, God lives and works within us."

I think it's interesting that he remembers that night as an important event during his time in the military; and, though it's perhaps ironic considering the circumstances, one of the things he learned while he was in the Marines was that God truly does work in mysterious ways. For whatever effect that late night conversation may have had on the others, he was fully aware of God's presence in his life and open to the wonder of how He would choose to use him.

It was not long after that time that my master completed his tour. I bet you can imagine how excited he was to be heading north to be rejoined with his family. Perhaps, too, you can imagine how he must have felt about starting a new job and wondering just what God had in store for him next.

Chapter Six

For he has rescued us from the dominion of darkness and brought us into the kingdom of the Son he loves. Colossians 1:13

My master has mentioned that when anyone in the Marines or the Navy gets the opportunity to go into town off-base or off-ship, most will get rid of their military garb and don their civvies. That's their nickname for civilian clothing, and putting on their civvies is almost always a cause for celebration among Marines and sailors. After completing two years of military service as a draftee, my friend arrived at that point where he could go back to the world and put on his civvies fulltime. Without a doubt, he was very happy to see that day arrive.

In January he received his honorable discharge and returned to his hometown to be with his wife and two children in their new home. It was amazing how spacious that apartment, with its two bedrooms, seemed after their military trailer. But their housing wasn't the only change for the family; for upon his return, though he couldn't have imagined it then, he also began what would turn out to be a forty-year career within the same organization. He has certainly wondered if God planned this all out for him, and I've heard him say more than once that he thinks that He did. He also believes that God had a tremendous influence in giving him those two years in the Marines as a step in his preparation for what turned out to be a long and wonderful career.

Part of the training for his civilian job was the discipline he learned as a Marine about staying at things and never giving up. Another valuable aspect of that training was the military belief in leading and leading by example. In addition, he had learned about the importance of being positive and looking forward, no matter what happened; even tactical withdrawals were sometimes necessary in order to go in a new direction. All in all he believed that he had done a good job being a Marine; and at the same time, he recognized how much he had benefited and what he had gotten in return. I've often heard him say that many times in business, as in life, you need to take the negative and turn it into a positive. He admits that following that philosophy can be difficult sometimes, and yet he also thinks it's at the core of any success that he had in his civilian career. It all makes me think that my buddy really did learn a lot during his stint in the Marines.

Soon after the family was rejoined, they settled happily into the pattern of life in Small-town, USA. It was good to be back where they had started with all the familiar places and people. The next several years were incredibly busy for both my master and his wife, and those years were filled with major events. They didn't stay long in the apartment they had rented for their return; for as soon as they could, they purchased their first home, a row house near where my friend had been raised. That house was replaced in a few years with a cozy Cape Cod that was located in a newer section right next to their children's elementary school. But by far the most important event during these years occurred when it was time to get ready to welcome the third child into their growing family.

This birth was to take place in their community hospital that, unlike the military facility where their daughters had been born, welcomed fathers into the birth experience. My buddy was anticipating sharing in this miracle with his wife by being with her in the delivery room, but unforeseen complications with the birth changed their plan. After they went through several scary and intense hours, you can imagine their complete joy when they were blessed by the safe arrival of their son David. With the birth of this wonderful baby boy who joined his beautiful big sisters, their family was now complete

During this busy time as a family man, my friend was also focusing full-time on his career. The maturity he had gained in the Marines and the loving responsibility of his family made him highly motivated. He worked hard during the day at his job, moving steadily up through the ranks of responsibility. As part of his career, he also took advantage of the education option that his company offered him and went to night school and took enough courses to obtain a graduate diploma over a ten-year period. This degree was highly focused on his particular industry; in addition, he had the opportunity to go to a major university and take an executive development course. He always thought that course was one of the best things he did educationally. Over this time, he continued to move his career towards the next step up, one rewarding step after another.

Spiritually this was also an important time of growth for my master's family. After they had returned to their hometown, one of the first things that he and Judy went back to was how important it was to exercise their faith and belief in a community of other believers. Soon after they were reestablished, they began to go to church and take their children to Sunday school. It was not long before they became deeply involved in their church and worship service. After several years, he was asked if he would be interested in helping with the church youth group.

By then he was already teaching the high school Sunday school class and thought that it was probably a good thing to become involved with the youth group that was made up of predominantly high school students with some junior high aged young people as well. On weekends and Wednesday nights he immersed himself in offering these teenagers the sharing of his faith. He continued working with those young people for eight years and remembers those times as a wonderful experience from which he thinks he probably grew, spiritually speaking, as much as and possibly more than his young charges.

During those eight years the group took three mission trips. The first was to Oklahoma where they delivered a van to a missionary on a Cherokee Indian reservation; they spent ten days there running a vacation Bible school for the children of the reservation and building a carport to house the van that they had purchased and delivered to the missionary. The second trip was to a thrift shop in Maine where a minister in a very economically depressed area had started a shop to sell used clothing and furniture. It also provided employment for some of the local people.

On that mission they didn't run a vacation Bible school, but they did totally repaint a barn and shop; they also added on to the shop with restrooms and a dressing room. The third trip was to Kentucky where one of the churches had been flooded; the group cleaned and repainted the entire building, both inside and outside. As he relates the stories of these trips, I can tell that they will always hold special memories for him.

It was around this time that several people in the community approached him and asked if he had ever thought about running for a position on the local school board. Though he had never considered the possibility before, they were able to convince him. My friend remembers that it was interesting running for that school board seat because it forced him to do and learn a lot of new things; and some of those old fears of the darkness in the attic came into his mind because it was a new venture, a new experience. But on the other side there was the fact that he could focus himself on learning about education at a time when it was so important in the lives of his children. He also learned quite a bit about interacting with different people and how to make things work in a group.

There were nine people on the school board from one community, bringing different points of view into the discussions that would impact all of the children and taxpayers that they represented. He has often said that serving on the school board was a real challenge, for it meant dealing with people's two most sensitive issues: their children and their wallets. The value of striving to do the best and right things, efficiently and effectively, is one of the most important things that he tried to contribute. He was fortunate enough to serve for two four-year terms on the school board and was eventually elected president; but as he came down to the end of his second term and was confronted with the decision of whether he should continue or not, he decided for several reasons not to go for reelection. One of the main factors was that he had just been named president of his company.

If you ask me, it's pretty amazing that after starting at the bottom rung of the ladder, he had worked hard enough and learned enough that he had achieved and earned the top job in a major organization in his community. So there he was in his civvies, nineteen years out of the Marines, with an extremely rewarding career that he could never have foreseen when he was back in the barracks. To this day, he believes that all of his other experiences along the way helped prepare him for this new and important career move. I've heard him say many times how he can't begin to say enough about how the Marine Corps prepared him. And he recognizes, too, that having spent eight years being the church youth coordinator and Sunday school teacher also prepared him, as did his two terms on the school board.

From a worldly sense, when he was named president of his company, he had reached the pinnacle of success. He had a family of three fine, thriving children and a wonderful wife; and he was earning a good salary in a highly responsible job. I heard one of my master's friends say recently that his was a true All-American success story. From the small-town boy to the Marine recruit to the entry-level employee, he had worked his way to the top. Everything in his life seemed absolutely perfect. Who could ask for more? But then there is another thread to his story, one that had been taking place all through the good times and all through the successes. It, too, has been a very real part of his journey.

To get a full understanding of this part of my friend's story, I guess we need to go back a bit to when he was a boy. From the time he was young, actually in third grade, he had needed to wear glasses. Like many children, his near-sightedness first showed up when he had trouble seeing the blackboard at school. As I mentioned before, there were times as an athlete that he had to accommodate what he then took to be fairly normal vision problems. Then there were those times in the Marines. Remember when he shot those perfect rounds into the wrong target, and then how about when he knocked down his drill instructor because he just wasn't seeing things quite right? But nobody thought too much of any of these incidents.

My master himself, only ever seeing out of his own eyes, had no idea that he really didn't have completely normal vision. He had passed all the military medical tests, and his own eye doctor never saw anything unusual except that he needed to wear glasses. But then when he was twenty-five, home from the Marines and getting established in his new job, he visited his eye doctor for what he thought was a routine check-up. He hadn't been noticing any particular problems, but it was time to get his eyeglass prescription checked. It was, he thought, to be a perfectly ordinary visit. But then his optometrist examined him. Without saying anything about what he suspected, he looked a little closer.

What the doctor saw was that his patient was developing cataracts. Now I don't know how much you know about cataracts, but that doctor was pretty surprised to see them in the eyes of such a young man. He sent him on to see an ophthalmologist, that's a medical doctor who specializes in diseases and surgery of the eye. The ophthalmologist saw the same problem and considered the possibilities of what could cause cataracts in someone so young. He ordered tests for my friend to see if he had diabetes or some other condition that could produce this condition, but all the tests came out fine. At that time, the doctor just wasn't sure what was going on; but since his patient was in otherwise perfect health, he suggested that they wait awhile and see what might happen.

Over the next couple of years, my master started noticing some problems; he occasionally was bumping into things or not seeing that there was something in his path. He also had a minor car accident that raised his concern because he was sure he hadn't seen what was about to happen. He decided then that it was time to go back for another check up.

At this visit, the eye doctor thought he knew what might be going on; and he told my friend that he suspected that he might have a condition called retinitis pigmentosa. He recommended that he go to Wills Eye Hospital, an excellent facility in Philadelphia that specializes in visual problems, to verify what he thought was happening. At first my buddy tried to make a little joke, as he often does to lighten a moment.

"So what does that mean?" he asked. "Are my eyes allergic to pigs?"

The doctor smiled but then explained that retinitis pigmentosa, often called RP, is an inherited eye disease that causes degeneration of the retina, which is light sensitive tissue that lines the inside of the eye. It's the retina that receives the images that we see and helps transmit them to the brain. As the disease progresses, it damages the retina and causes a gradual decline in the ability to see. The doctor also explained the mystery of the presence of cataracts in such a young man as being nature's way of trying to protect his eyes from ultraviolet light and that he believed they were connected to the R.P. As they continued to talk, the doctor added there was no way to predict how his vision would be affected in the future because the visual changes had been so gradual. He never mentioned the word *blind*.

Not long ago my master was talking with a friend about RP; and he asked him how he felt when he first got the diagnosis, thinking that the answer would be that he was terribly upset or angry. Part of my friend's answer seemed to surprise him. I'll let you see what you think.

"As I left the doctor's office, I was trying to absorb what he had told me; and even though he had never said 'You are going blind,' it seemed, from what he did say, that he thought that eventually I would lose my vision from the peripheral to the center. I know I was feeling numb at that point and that I didn't fully understand all of the implications of the disease. I think it's sort of like knowing that, hey, someday we're all going to die; but when you're in your twenties, death doesn't feel as if it's going to be happening anytime soon. You certainly hope not, and you tend to push any thoughts of your own death away. I think in my own mind that day, I was still trying to absorb the fact that my vision was going to gradually get worse and possibly the word blind was in my mind, but it just didn't feel real to me. I had only ever known one person who was blind, so it just didn't connect to anything I knew. I guess you could say that I was feeling pretty somber, but mostly unsure of what it all meant or could mean in the future.

"I decided to try to put it out of my mind and continue with my plan for the day which was to visit my friend in the hospital. He was a young man just a little older than I was. He was in the hospital for something that didn't seem too serious; in fact he was supposed to be leaving the hospital soon, but I wanted to be sure to stop in and see him while he was there.

"I remember getting in the car and driving up the road toward the hospital, looking around me, seeing the scenery and all of the beauty, you know, the sky and the trees and sunlight, and wondered how long I would still have those pleasures. I also thought if blindness is the result of this condition and if it happens when I'm still young enough to be working fulltime, what will it mean to my family, what will it mean to my career, what will happen with all the things I love that require sight? But then I thought, there's nothing I can do about it. Truthfully, none of it seemed quite real; it seemed so distant, so abstract... because that day I could see.

"By the time I got to the hospital, I had made myself stop thinking about the visit to the doctor and all of the unknowns that I had no way to control. I made my way to my friend's room, and we talked and laughed for a little while. He seemed just like his usual self, and I thought he was doing pretty well.

"But as I went to leave, he stopped me and said, If something happens to me, will you help my wife?'

"I answered right away that he was going to be fine. But he insisted, and I reassured him, still saying that he was soon going to be going home and that everything was absolutely all right. A few days later I received a phone call from the hospital. Unfortunately, my friend had been tragically correct, for his condition had worsened beyond anything the doctors could do to save him. I immediately went to the hospital to offer my prayers and whatever comfort I could to his wife.

"Considering the loss of my friend and the tragic effect it had on his family, the doctor's diagnosis of my RP just didn't seem all that important."

"So if that diagnosis wasn't important, what is?" his friend asked, "to live each day as if it's our last? To live each day as if today is the day that we believe the Lord will return?"

"Yes, that would be a great way to live each day and not be anxious about anything. But in reality, we usually wake up in the morning feeling at least a little anxiety about what's ahead. So how do we start each day, how do we get through it? Where can we truly place our trust? I think the answer is that we must trust each other and in God. And, when trust is shaken or damaged, what then? Prayer? Yes, that helps. But walking through each day is always a challenge. I think that must be true for everyone."

Chapter Seven

Do not be anxious about anything, but in everything, by prayer and petition, with thanksgiving, present your requests to God. And the peace of God, which transcends all understanding, will guard your hearts and your minds in Christ Jesus. Philippians 4:6 and 7

Because R.P. can be so unpredictable, neither my friend nor his doctor could fully anticipate the path that the disease might take. After looking back across his earlier vision differences, it seemed possible that it had always been a factor in his life. The problems, fortunately, had been relatively slight; and the worsening of his vision was so gradual that it had never had any impact on his actions or decisions. After all, he had lived all of his boyhood and his early years as an adult with the complete belief that he was fully sighted. Whatever small accommodations he had needed to make along the way had never had any major effect on his being an athlete, a Marine, a loving husband and father, and a highly successful climber of the corporate ladder. In those early days after the diagnosis, he tried to focus on the present and not dwell too much on what might happen in the future.

He did decide to follow his doctor's advice and go to Wills Eye Hospital to confirm the diagnosis and see if there was anything that they could do to help him. The ophthalmologists there carried out a series of tests. They put dye in his veins and then took photographs of his retina to measure what was actually going on inside his eyes, and they did other tests with a lot of sophisticated equipment. It was a long day as both specialists and residents examined him and studied the test results. I've heard my friend talk about that visit, and some of the things he learned.

"At the end of the day, I was sitting in an office waiting for the head doctor to come in to talk with me about what he had found, and the group of residents that had been following what was going on was waiting with me. One of them seemed to be the leader, and he started talking with me; from what he said, I could tell he was indirectly confirming the diagnosis. Then he asked me if I understood what it all meant.

"'I think I do,' I told him. 'Gradually, over time, I might lose my sight. '"

"'There's no way to determine when or even if that will happen,' he explained. 'It could be that your vision will never get any worse than it is today, or it could deteriorate more quickly than we could possibly anticipate. Do you know of anyone else, any family members who have R.P.?'" he asked.

"'I really don't. I've never heard anybody in my family talk about a relative who's gone blind. Does it matter if someone else has had the same thing? '"

"'Only in that if there is a family history, someone you're related to, we would have a possible timeline. But even if that were the case, it wouldn't be an accurate predictor because R.P. doesn't always follow predictable patterns. '"

"At that point, the head doctor joined us and discussed with me some of the test results. Whatever small hope I'd had of an incorrect diagnosis by my regular ophthalmologist was put to rest. Gathering my courage, I turned to the doctor and asked the biggest question that was on my mind, 'Does this mean I am going blind? '"

"'Not necessarily and there's no way to know because the effects of R.P. are so different for each person. Many people with the same condition go their whole lives with at least some vision. It just isn't something that we're able to predict. '"

When my master told this story he added, "In my experience, all ophthalmologists that I've known avoid the word *blind*. I think it's like a defeat for them that they just don't want to say; and because they work every day to help people maintain and improve their sight, I can certainly understand that."

Before he left Wills Eye Hospital, the doctor and residents told him some ways he could accommodate for the reduction in peripheral vision, like being sure to use two mirrors on the car when he was driving. Then they told him that he would know when accommodating wasn't enough. That comment really hit him when he was driving home that day, and he began to think seriously about the impact of having to give up things and the effect it would have on his life.

The first real indications that he needed to make some adjustments began when he was twenty-seven, and the cataracts were starting to take their toll. He first mainly noticed the impact of the changes as an athlete. While establishing his family and his career, even with his church and community activities, he had continued to make time whenever he could for sports. Being an athlete was an important part of who he was and how he saw himself, and the physical activity renewed and energized him for all that he had going on in his life. When he returned from the Marines, he got back into playing the hardball and softball that he loved. But as his vision diminished, he relegated himself to just playing softball. Also in that time he taught himself, with a little bit of help from others, how to throw underhand; so that most of the time he played first base rather than pitching as he had done before.

By the end of his sporting days, he also learned how to play a fairly good game of tennis; and he had always dabbled a little in the game of golf. Though these sports were not the most important thing in his life, they were fun activities that he enjoyed; and as I mentioned, sports provided a good balance and physical outlet that enriched the other parts of his life. It might be a little hard for anyone who has never been an athlete to understand how these forced accommodations to his visual changes must have felt; but for someone that had always really been into athletics, it could not have been a completely easy adjustment.

Slowly but surely over the next few years, my friend's vision continued to narrow. He became increasing aware that he was seeing less, that the field of his vision was becoming smaller; and his problems became even worse at night. He knew that he needed to be more and more cautious in all of his day-to-day activities. Though he sought out the best medical care he could find, even traveling to

Boston to see specialists there, he had to start to accept the fact that there was simply no cure for RP. He began to believe that his vision was likely to continue to diminish and that even the best doctors in the field had no treatment that could stop the condition's progress.

Not long ago I heard someone who knows the depth of my master's faith, ask him if his growing awareness of his loss of vision had made him angry with God.

He told his friend, with all sincerity, "During this time I never stopped believing in Jesus as my Savior. But in my obedient walk, I always held back a little piece here or a little piece there, always wandering a little bit to the left or the right, always allowing the darkness of my heart to coexist with His spirit. And that will bring fear. Just like in the attic when as a boy I flipped the light switch off and coexisted in the darkness of the fears of the imaginary creatures, in my heart I sometimes flipped the switch off and allowed the darkness of my imaginings to coexist."

Then he added, "No, I've never been angry with God for my blindness; my faith and complete trust in Him and His intended path for me have never wavered. I've always accepted and believed that God has a reason for everything, and it is my responsibility to learn to live well and faithfully within His intent for me. Yet, at the same time, I'm very grateful that I hadn't known earlier than I did about what was ahead because I wouldn't have wanted to have changed anything that came before in my life."

At that his friend kind of shook his head, "That is amazing to me. It's hard of course to know how you might feel when you haven't experienced something yourself, but I think I might have needed to shake my fist at heaven and asked, 'Why me?'"

The next major concession to the deterioration of his vision, and one that had a number of other consequences concerned my buddy's ability to drive a car. He had learned to drive as a teenager; and as it is with most boys, it was a real rite of passage for him. Being a driver had provided that wonderful world of independence and freedom that almost everyone appreciates. It also had opened his social world as a teen to venturing beyond his small town; and, of course, it was considered crucial in those days for dating. Driving also had given him a certain status when he was one of the few Marines on his base who had a car; he was the one who provided transportation for shopping and those all-important trips to the hospital when the young women that he and his wife knew were ready to have their babies.

But the time came when this seasoned, competent driver started experiencing some problems. These difficulties actually started occurring before he knew from the doctors what was happening. I think it's probably best to let him tell the story as I heard him relay it. In that same conversation about whether he had been angry with God, he talked about some of the changes he had to make as he started to face the fact that he was no longer seeing as well as he once had.

"I remember having two accidents, fender benders, and those relatively small incidents helped me make that important decision to give up my driver's license. One happened on a night we were leaving a drive-in movie theater that emptied onto a major highway. I looked around for a safe time to pull out on to the road, and I completely missed seeing a car that was coming and caused an accident. Similar things nearly happened a couple more times. I thought about these near misses a lot, and I tried driving even more carefully. Giving up driving was a terribly hard realization to face, and for a while I really struggled with the decision.

"Then I had another fender bender, and it helped me to decide what I had to do. I had pulled up to an intersection and failed to see a car coming from my right; and thinking the road was clear, I pulled out in front of that car. Fortunately, neither of us was moving fast and the other driver was making a turn into the street where I had been stopped. Even more fortunately, because of our reduced speed no one was injured; but it hit me that day: what if the car had been a bicycle with a child on it? I then thought, I have to stop this; by the grace of God, no one had ever gotten hurt, and yet I knew that I had been given the signal that I must lay this down."

He went on to say, "But you know, when I had to give up driving a car and some of my sports, in one way it presented the opportunity for me to be more focused on my career. Also, not being able to drive a car made me depend on other people. I've learned a lot about both others and myself through being dependent on them. Out of all this I think I grew."

Now I guess you might be wondering what effect all of these changes might have had on my master's family. The first thing I'm going to tell you is that I think the best decision he ever made was choosing the wife that he did. It almost makes you wonder how that inexperienced teenaged guy could have been so wise when he asked Judy the big question. For when those two kids said, "For better or worse...In sickness and in health," they really meant it. I think, too, that it's a very good thing that she's as secure in her beliefs as her husband has always been because, like him, she has never seen her husband's blindness as any reason to doubt or question her faith.

Let's be honest, it couldn't have been an easy thing for that young woman, no matter how good and wise she is, to have faced the fact that her healthy, robust, active young husband had a serious eye condition, one that could result in blindness. It certainly couldn't have been easy for her to stand by as he had to make the necessary adjustments in his life, especially when many of those adjustments had a direct effect on her life, as well. Just consider the fact that once he gave up his license, she became the main driver for all of them. That in itself must have been a real change in the life of an already very busy mom, for that decision meant that she would be doing all the errands, driving the children to their events, and, at the same time, providing transportation for her husband much of the time for his work and other involvements. But Judy accepted what couldn't be changed; and I think that only he knows the full extent of the total support and help she has always been to him.

I've watched how much she does for him every day, but even I didn't realize the extent of all she needed to do until, just the other day, I heard her talking with her good friend Alice. My buddy had settled in to listening to a baseball game on television, and I knew he wouldn't need me for quite awhile. I decided to see how Judy was doing, and I found her at the kitchen table talking with her friend over a cup of tea. I lay down beside Judy and she patted my head in her nice way. I guess my presence in the room made Alice think about my master's blindness.

"I was thinking the other day about all that I do at home, and then I thought about you. I know how much work I do and how much I try to help my husband and kids, but I can't imagine what it must be like for you," Alice said.

Judy laughed a little before answering, "I think we all just do what it takes. It might be different for other marriages and families, but I think we all go about what needs to be done whatever our circumstances."

"But aren't there things that you do to help John that most of us never think about?" Alice asked. "I certainly don't mean to pry at all, but I have wondered about this."

"Goodness, I know you're not prying, and I guess I probably do need to help out a little more than many wives."

"What was it like in the beginning?" Alice asked. "How did you feel when you knew John was going to be blind?"

"Actually, it all happened so gradually. The real changes took place over several years; I guess we made the adjustments kind of one day at a time. The hardest part was seeing how frustrated he would get. And to tell you the truth, a lot of times the frustrations seemed to be directed at me."

"Isn't that always the way," Alice commented. "We always seem to take out things most on the ones we love the most. It isn't very fair, I know. But it just seems to be how it is. Maybe it's because we trust the other person so much. But I'm thinking about all the regular stuff like meals and clothes. How did you work that out?"

"As I said, it all happened pretty gradually. I remember when I began picking out John's clothes when I went shopping. Then I started laying out his things every night to make sure that they worked together. Even when I'm going to be away, I make sure that he has an outfit hanging on the closet door. Over time I got it to a kind of system. You know, little things, like for a long time I've only bought him black socks, so he wouldn't end up with things clashing. His belts are always smooth for one color, textured for another. And he mostly only has white dress shirts."

"It sounds as if you really thought it out," Alice agreed.

"Well, you know he's always needed to be dressed well for work and meetings, and I wouldn't want him to be embarrassed. Actually, one day he came home from lunch and had on two different color shoes. I guess that was when I knew I needed to arrange things a little better. As for meals, that has never been much of an issue. John has never had any problem eating; all I need to do is arrange the food on his plate and tell him where things are. That's never been a problem. It all made me a better housekeeper, too. When I realized that having things lying around could make him trip, I knew it was time to keep everything neater in the house. But none of that has ever mattered as much to me as how frustrated he can get."

"What do you mean?"

"It was so hard for him to give things up. He used to love to drive. Once he had to move over to the passenger seat, it was pretty upsetting to him. And, of course, there were those times when he was sure I wasn't driving right, or at least not like he would. That would cause some tense moments for both of us. Even mowing the lawn. He used to love that job. Once he couldn't do it and I started, that would sometimes frustrate him, too."

"Gosh," said Alice, "I can't believe I never saw any of this. It must have been so hard for you. I can't believe you haven't ever seemed sorry for yourself."

"I've never felt that way. Truthfully, I never have. I've sometimes felt bad for him though. I could see what was happening. Some days he's come home with a rip on his pants or a cut on his chin or head from running into something, and those kinds of accidents can make me feel a lot of pain for him. I recognize his helplessness sometimes, but then I know he's never been helpless. The stubbornness that I've sometimes been subject to has overall been a good thing in him. I don't mean to say it's always been a graceful transition. It hasn't been, and that's for sure; but I always know how it must be for him. Even when I'm hurt by feeling as if his frustration has been unfairly directed at me, I know what he must be feeling, too."

"I can't believe how unselfish you've been. I honestly mean that," Alice said.

"The most important thing," Judy answered, "the very most important thing is that, even though we both had to change some things in our lives, in every other way, John is the exact same man that I chose to marry."

Once I heard those reassuring words, I decided to go back to the living room to see how our team was doing. But there was a commercial on and my mind wandered to some things Judy had said, and I realized that I've noticed times he has been frustrated, too. One of the first things that comes to mind happens because of the way people talk. They'll say something like, "What you want to do is go over there," and they may even be pointing. Or they'll say, "Sit here," when it would be helpful if they would say, "It's about three feet in front of you," or if they would pat the chair so he could hear where they mean.

I've also heard him talk about how he's lost the advantage of body language in conversations. Even we dogs can tell a lot from people's expressions and the way they stand or move, so I can understand that not seeing those details would be tough sometimes. He wouldn't even know if someone is happy or sad unless the person's words or voice would tell him. I think these different frustrations can make him feel a little alone sometimes. I've seen, too, how upset he can get when he walks into things, like a door or a drawer that's left part way open when he's not expecting it. Almost always his reactions to these things are momentary, but I can see how they affect him. I've heard people at The Seeing Eye say an expression, something like, "Ain't Being Blind a Pain?" and I guess that's part of what they mean.

I've noticed that sometimes when he bumps into people or touches someone in a place he never intended it makes him feel embarrassed and he apologizes right away. Or he might get frustrated when he's alone and needs to find something and just can't. Yes, there are lots of little day-to-day things that can be hard for him; but honestly, I think almost all of the time he doesn't let the little stuff get him down. I think he and Judy do just fine almost all of the time.

But what about those three beautiful children that these two were raising in those transition years? When the fact of his vision change really started having its effect, this young couple was approaching their thirties. Their two little girls were going to school right next to their home, and their baby son was quickly changing into a very active little boy. My master and his wife talk about how they fully understood and enjoyed their responsibilities to help each of the children grow and learn to understand the world; and they readily assumed the importance of supporting them in their various directions.

They also helped them to understand why they were different from their sister or brother and the significance of recognizing and loving their own uniqueness. Perhaps most importantly, they taught them about God and His Son and the importance of faith in their growth and happiness. It's likely, too, that all three of the kids grew up with and still have in their early memories the understanding that their Dad had a visual impairment. But even as they knew that fact, life for them was actually very normal. I've heard Judy say that she thinks that growing up with their dad's blindness taught them all an extra measure of patience and cooperation. It seems to me that they were good things for them to learn, and it certainly speaks to the love that all of them have always shared.

I've heard people talk about the innocence and acceptance that children have and their unquestioning ability to think that everything is okay because they know they can trust their parents. In this family, though they knew something of their father's vision difficulties, it didn't have, as far as anyone could tell, a significant impact on their sense of security. As I've heard my friend say, when you're a child you don't sit around hoping that dad pays the electric bill or that mom puts food in the refrigerator; those things are taken for granted out of trust and love. As parents you just do your best no matter what adversity you might be facing, and you don't let the children know whether or not you're worried about those things that are adult concerns.

I've also heard my master compare the trust of a child for her parent as the way God wants us to accept and trust in Him. He refers to the verse in Proverbs, in which it says: "Trust in the Lord and lean not on your own understanding." In Sunday school one day this verse was discussed, and it was explained that God wants people to see that they need to trust and believe that He has everything under control. It sounds to me as if God told everyone to have faith in Him just like the faith of a child.

My friend was fortunate that he was able to drive a car and live for the most part a very normal, visually acute life until around the time that each of the girls reached the age of sixteen. When it was time for them to drive, and time for a father to teach them how to drive, he was facing the possibility of having to give up his own driver's license. When Kelly was sixteen, he still had a license. He always says that he taught her how to drive legally, and he taught Kris how to drive not quite so legally. In between their learning to drive and getting licenses, he had turned his own in and stopped driving himself.

For David, being younger than his sisters by a few years, the need to understand his dad's diminishing sight started earlier in his life. At a recent holiday dinner, I heard my master and his son reliving some good memories. I was settled quietly under the table not making a sound, but I have to tell you that if I'd been a person this story would really have made me laugh just like they were.

It seems they were walking from their home into town to the local five and ten. My friend was explaining to his son that they were walking because it was a good thing to do but also because he wasn't able to drive. That led to David's asking questions about his father's vision. Looking for a way to explain, his dad answered that his eye condition was genetic and that it existed in his genes.

In all innocence, David looked up at him and asked, "Well Dad, why don't you just change your pants?"

But even though he was younger when he needed to understand what was happening than his sisters were, David enjoyed all of the normal boy activities with his father. Among other things, they've always shared the same love for baseball and played it a lot together. My friend continued to throw with his son pretty much until he was through high school. I have heard him say, though, that he did switch from hardballs to tennis balls for their sessions, so that when David threw the ball back to him and he didn't see it, it didn't hurt quite so much.

While we're thinking about those great kids, you might be wondering about their eyes and their vision. Because RP, as my master tried to explain to David, is a genetic disease, you can imagine how reassured and relieved their parents were when they had the children tested and learned that they did not and would not have the same condition. They were told that genetic diseases can be pretty unpredictable. Much, much later they were to learn that their grandchildren were also spared the gene. But that good news is jumping way too far ahead.

It was around this time, probably a good fifteen years after my friend had left the Marines and had settled into our hometown, that the family decided to go on a trip that included going back to the Marine Corps base where my friend had served. They were then going to travel on to Wilmington, North Carolina, and from there they planned to swing west to visit Judy's sister and her husband and their three daughters. My buddy and his wife were very excited to revisit the place where they had spent the first two years of their lives together and where the girls had been born. They thought that their daughters would share in the wonder and enthusiasm of visiting their birthplace now that they were teenagers.

But as it often is with kids, especially teenagers, they didn't think it was a big deal. Actually, once they got there, they found out that the hospital where the girls had been born had been closed as part of the scaling down of the military after the Vietnam War. It just wasn't very exciting for them to see their birthplace as a boarded up building. The base, too, had changed; and the kids, understandably, weren't able to appreciate those early days of their parents' lives. But, in spite of the changes, their parents did appreciate returning to the place where so much had happened for them.

They next went down to Wilmington, North Carolina where there was a battleship tour with a pretty fantastic light show at night. They had a hotel room across the harbor, and they had just seen the light show with all the booming and flash. When it was time for settling in for the night, my master and his wife had a double bed and the children were going to sleep in a pull out bed. Just as the three kids simultaneously got in, the contraption folded itself right back up and had them all semi trapped in a V position. When they remember this story together, they all end up laughing; fortunately, no one had been hurt but it was a great funny time. As it sometimes goes, that bed story holds more memories than any other part of their trip.

Chapter Eight

Trust in the Lord with all your heart and lean not on your own understanding. Proverbs 3:5

From a worldly sense, by the time he was forty and had been named president of his company, my master had reached the pinnacle of success. He was earning a good salary, more than he had ever thought would be possible when he started his career. His two daughters were in college and his son was in high school, and all three of them were thriving. It was around this time that the family was planning to move into a larger house in a new neighborhood that was being built right outside of their town; it was a good move because it was close to his office and would allow him to walk to work. Within both his community and his company, he had a respected position; and that journey in his career would even take him from being the big fish in the little pond in his small town company to also becoming involved with a job-related trade association at the state level where he became chairman.

He served on several other boards in the community where they successfully put together a town revitalization program. He also volunteered at his church where they restructured the finances and accomplished some other projects. He was involved, too, in fund raising for various organizations. All these things were good works, and he truly believed he was helping people. He was even asked to speak several times at different places within his state and as far away as California and Canada. On some occasions, much to his delight, he was asked to sing solos at some of those conferences and in churches. Life was good. Life was very good; and this big fish from a little pond, by all worldly measures, had become a success.

Yet, at the same time, he remained aware of what it means to be a success. For he has never forgotten that there is more than one definition of that word. The first kind of success can be measured by the things of this world; and in this regard, many tend to see it as the amount of money people have, their position in their work, the size of their home, or the number of things they possess. Yet to my friend those things are not what real success is about. For him, it is when we have developed our relationship with God to the point that we walk with Him and He allows our relationships with others to be part of that walk.

As he looks back now and thinks of all that he was doing when he was at that pinnacle, it must sound as if he was a highly disciplined, active individual. Actually, that's exactly what he was. But I've also heard him talk about the fact that there was always another piece to him, a piece that had to do with vision; for he admits that he has often been easily distracted by the beautiful things in this world.

One evening my master was talking with a friend who asked him what he missed most when he became blind after having been sighted, and this question started quite a long discussion which I think shows that even at the height of success, my friend must have been struggling for some answers. He responded to his friend's question by saying that being able to drive a car and being able to play sports were two things he really missed, and he added with a smile that the third thing was the ability to observe a beautiful woman walking down the street. Then he went on to wonder aloud if all of these things are part of a darkness in the heart? And he recognized that they can be. His explanation was that if you dwell on any one of those things, if you dwell on just wanting to drive a car or if you dwell on just wanting to play sports, if they are more important than anything else around you, then they become a kind of blind ambition.

He then suggested that while there is the darkness of blindness, there can be an even more fearful darkness that can exist within one's own heart. This comment led both men into talking about their thoughts about fear and darkness. They agreed that, if the distractions of this world take your concentration away from those things that are important and interfere with the relationships you have with your wife, your family, or your business associates, than those distractions are a true darkness. He went on to say that physical blindness is a negative but that overall he has been able to keep a positive spin on it. You know, that old Marine philosophy of his about turning the negative into a positive.

"But the truth is," he added, "That there is no advantage to darkness. It truly is a pain, and I think now that the fear I had of the darkness as a child had to do with the unknowns that surrounded me; and yet for the most part the things I had feared were non-existent. Being blind is like that, it is always being in the dark and not knowing what is around you and having natural concerns and fears about what might be there, always stepping out with caution, living with caution, while at the same time trying to compete in the fully sighted world. I think the darkness in our hearts has to do with the inability to feel good about what's ahead and have confidence in it."

Then he went on to say that he believes that the darkness of being blind is far less of a problem than that which can exist within our hearts.

When his friend asked him what he meant by that, he explained, "I know about that kind of blackness, too. For whether we're sighted or whether we are blind, I'm afraid that we all have a natural bent to darkness in our hearts. For each of us it may take on different manifestations. For some it might be ambition; you've heard of people who have blind ambition. For some it might be the desire to accumulate great wealth to the point that it blinds them to all and anything else. It might be for the attainment of power to the extent where control is the most important thing, and the person is blind to whatever might be around them. In essence, I think what we actually have is that the darkness in our heart results from our undisciplined desire to attain some one thing at the cost of everything else."

Then he paused before adding, "Jesus said, 'What does it profit a man if he gains the whole world but loses his soul?' These words should help us see that we should have a full vision of all that's around us and not be blinded by any one desire."

To me at least this conversation says something about humans, including my friend. It seems that however you might define success in the people world, it, like so much else for them, includes some struggles. I would also guess that his advancing blindness had to have had some impact, even though I believe him when he talks about the other darkness being more dangerous. I have to believe that those years of worsening vision, between the time he learned about RP at twenty-seven and when he became president of his company at forty, had to have had an underside. For even as he was making those adjustments, first in sports and then with driving, his vision continued to deteriorate.

Except for the people who were closest to him, no one was too aware that anything was wrong. He just kept moving forward with his family, his work, his church, and community. Being tall and strong, with an impressive carriage, I would imagine that almost everyone he encountered thought of him as absolutely fine; and, of course except for his vision, he's always been a really healthy person. Making the transition to having the world know how much he really couldn't see must have been pretty tough.

I heard him talk at The Seeing Eye about the years when he was coming to terms with his loss of vision and he said, "R.P. is like a recurring disease; you can put it in perspective within the moment, especially during the time when you can still see and the possibility of blindness doesn't seem real. But then there is the recurring part of it. What happens is that you give up one thing at a time; and with each change it causes you to have some of the same feelings as the first diagnosis, but with each loss it's just that much more real. You grieve for the loss of each one thing until eventually you grieve the loss of all of the light. This recurring grieving finally culminates in being blind. I guess it gets down to going through each day as a challenge, to feel the inevitable sorrow but, at the same time, still claim joy, to keep refocusing on the good in your life."

I heard him tell a story once that I think reveals something of what this must have been like for him, especially when he knew the likely consequence of what he had been experiencing.

"Soon after leaving the school board and becoming president of the company, I had decided to try the use of a cane and got some instruction from a professional social worker who was trained in mobility and orientation. I remember when I first ordered my cane and it came to my office in a box, I set it in the corner. And there it sat for about a month. I was really fearful of beginning to use it, that white cane with the red tip, that would let everybody know that, well, they'd know that I was becoming blind. After having the cane sitting in the box in the corner all that time, one day when everybody else had left the office, I got it out, looked at it awhile, then stuffed it back in the box, and returned it to the corner. It sat there for another month or so again; and then a day came when everyone else had left the office, and I went to the corner and I carried the box with the cane in it to my home.

"I then set it in the corner of my office at home. Another month or so went by, and one day I took the cane out of the box and finally threw the box away; but I still didn't pick it up or try using it. I put it back in the corner. Finally after another few months, I began to use the cane at night, you know, when nobody would see me. But in actuality, it was important to begin to use it because I had been running into people accidentally in lobbies or crowded rooms, and it was becoming awkward to explain to them that I didn't see very well. But by having the cane, they would now know that there was a problem.

"Once I finally got enough courage to use it, it created another obstacle because people didn't know what to say. What do you say to the blind man with his cane in the corner? Often I would go to receptions before dinners and wind up standing in the corner, just me and my cane. Sure, some people would talk to me; but it seemed that white stick with the red point was almost off-putting to a lot of them."

I've got to say that the story of the cane makes me feel a little sad for my good friend. But then he has certainly never wanted anyone to feel bad for him. The other thing is that his experience with that cane was, I think, a hump he just had to get over. As painful as I'm sure it was, he had to come to terms with what was happening to him. I hope that doesn't sound insensitive, but the truth is that in a roundabout way that cane led to the part of his journey that I really like best. I'm pretty sure you'll see why.

Around this time, Judy, who was of course noticing what was taking place because of the struggle over using the cane, began to talk to him about whether or not he would ever consider looking into getting a guide dog. From the first, the whole idea made him fearful, for it was yet another new piece for him in his acknowledging his blindness. And, as hard as it is for me to believe it, I've actually heard him say that before he got his first Seeing Eye dog, he had never been a dog lover. The way he explains this astonishing fact is that the family in which he was raised had not had very many pets. From time to time they had pet rabbits, but having a pet rabbit is a lot different from having a dog or even a cat. For a pet rabbit, basically you provide a pen, feed it, and give it water, and that's about it. Once in awhile you might take it out and let it hop around the yard a little, and in some cases people might take it inside. But beyond a rabbit or two, his was not a family that had a lot of pets around; and they never had a dog.

After they were married, he learned very quickly that Judy is a true dog lover, having come from a family where there was always a pet dog; in her childhood experience, most of her beloved dogs were Boxers. Because of her love for pets, the family that my master and she created almost always had a pet dog and many times a cat or two, as well. I guess for the most part he kind of tolerated those pets. I'm sure it wasn't that he was ever mean to them, but he never had to take care of them. He didn't even feed them though occasionally he did help to bathe them.

The family pretty much always had a pet dog, including a German Shepherd that they only had a short time because that dog, I'm embarrassed to say, had total disrespect for Judy and she just couldn't control it. They also had an Irish Setter named Ember who gave the family six puppies, which they were able to distribute among their friends. From what I've heard, Ember was a good girl although it sounds as if she might have been a little short on focus. Then there was Kindle, their Golden Retriever; she's the family pet I've heard the most about. Wonderful Kindle is the dog that David often talks about; she was probably everyone's favorite pet and especially his. It sounds as if she was a very special girl; I would have liked to have known her. Late in life Kindle endured a lot of different problems from having to be treated for heartworm to needing a pin in her hip after being in a serious accident; but as far as being an obedient dog, she was top drawer.

About the time that my friend started to use a cane, the family lost that wonderful Kindle to the aging process. The next dog to be brought home was a black lab named Cisco who was the consummate alpha dog. He wanted to be in charge, totally in charge, of all of them. Though he did usually listen to my buddy, Cisco's bossiness and stubbornness did nothing to inspire him to want to take on a guide dog. But it was also during the time of Cisco that Judy and some others were growing more persistent in encouraging him to reconsider the idea. When he was finally convinced that he'd at least learn more, they began to research the possibility of using a guide dog.

Though they did look into several different schools that provide similar services, they finally settled on the organization called The Seeing Eye. It seemed to be the best option for a few reasons, including the fact that they allow you to take ownership of the dog, which isn't the case with all such organizations. They also found out that, though the actual cost for training and preparing the dog for service is probably close to an almost unfathomable fifty thousand dollars, your first dog from them only costs one hundred and fifty dollars and subsequent dogs only cost fifty. My master the businessman couldn't help but see that this was a great deal. The real clincher to the decision was that the Seeing Eye in Morristown, New Jersey, is only about an hour and a half away from the family's home, so they could get there quickly if the dog needed follow-up training for some reason.

Even after what he had learned, it would be a great overstatement to say that, during the time they were trying to make this decision, he was jumping for joy about sharing his life with a canine creature. The truth is, though it's still hard for me to believe, that he was very apprehensive about giving his trust to a dog. He was also concerned about having to groom a dog or give it medications or to have to constantly clean up after it. Let's face it, the whole prospect of bringing a creature into his life, one that he had never fully had to take care of before, was quite daunting to him.

Fortunately though, he had the opportunity to talk to some people at the Seeing Eye and to some other blind people who were using dogs. When he actually got to the Seeing Eye campus before making his decision, he was able to talk with instructors, as well as to people who were returning for their second or third or even fourth dogs. He could see in them their genuine excitement and their total belief in the independence and dignity that having a dog can give.

Intellectually, he was beginning to grasp the freedom he could experience and the reassurance that his wife and family would also feel in his having a guide dog. He finally decided that he was just going to have to overcome his fears and make that run across his attic and find out what all this could be about, and so he filled out the application. For although he was hesitant, he was extremely motivated to be as independent as he could possibly be. Even though he was still not fully convinced that this venture would work out, once he received the necessary approval that he was a good candidate, he started all of the many preparations at work and at home to take four weeks out of his life to go to the Seeing Eye to learn what this new adjustment would take...and to get a dog.

Fortunately, a gentleman that they knew about from a nearby town called my friend about a week before he was to leave and told him that he had just gotten his seventh dog from The Seeing Eye. This man, who had been blinded when he was young from meningitis, had just recently retired from teaching high school. He talked about what the Seeing Eye training entailed and what it would be like to live there for a month. He urged my master to take every opportunity to play with his dog and to pet it a lot. He had other good suggestions about making the best possible start during the training period. As it sometimes happens, this wonderful person whom he had never actually talked with before came into my friend's life at just the right moment and helped prepare him for this next transition in his life.

Soon the time came for the trip to Morristown. Judy drove him there on a bright Saturday morning; and even though she had enthusiastically encouraged the idea of a guide dog, she was feeling a lot of concern about her husband's being in training and away from home for a full month. She couldn't help but worry about all the things she did to help him function in his day-to-day living and whether anyone there would take the same interest in his welfare.

She had an opportunity to go into the building where the people in training stayed with their dogs, and she was reassured by the friendliness and kindness of the staff and favorably impressed by the facilities. But still, when it was time for her to leave, she felt a great deal of emotion. With tears in her eyes, she began the drive home. Then as she was leaving the grounds and about to enter the highway, she saw a doe standing still by the road. She stopped the car and looked at the deer as it gazed serenely at her. There was something truly extraordinary in that unspoken communication, and suddenly she felt a comforting peace about what lay ahead. For she knew then that everything would be all right.

"Thank you, Lord," she whispered with reverence. With a full heart, she continued her journey home.

Chapter Nine

Wait for the Lord; be strong and take heart and wait for the Lord. Psalm 27:14

Finally, after all of the doubt and debate, my master was at The Seeing Eye. Now I'm sure you can see why this part of his journey is so exciting to me. We can't jump ahead right now, though, to my being part of the story. Goodness, I wasn't even born at that time. But still, I can certainly relate to everything that happened during that first training session; and I'm going to let you in on a little secret that not even my buddy, my best-ever friend, knows. The secret is that I'm kind of glad I wasn't his first dog. He learned a great deal over the next several years before I became a part of his life that made things so easy for me. Since I feel both gratitude and respect for the good dogs that came before me, I am honored to be able to tell their stories and how they, too, were an important part of his life.

When my friend first arrived, he met his instructor and learned more about the facility that would be his home for the next month. He found out where his room and the lounge were and where he could do his laundry. Then he learned the route to that all-important place where they serve the meals. He also met the twenty other blind people; and five of them, like him, were there for their first dog. The rest of the group was returning for their second or fifth or even sixth dog. It might sound strange, but since the time he began confronting the truth of his lessening vision, it was his first exposure to a group of blind people.

Long before when he had gone to a Christian youth camp as a child there was a counselor who was blind, but he hadn't had a dog. In fact, he didn't even use a cane. He used what is called a sighted guide, that's a person who was with him and helped him all of the time. But this counselor was not fully employed and living in a sighted world. He lived at home with his parents, and his situation was very different from my master's who fully planned on continuing to live, work, and function in a totally sighted world. So getting to know the rest of his group of twenty, who were also working toward independence through the help of their dogs, was a totally new experience for him.

My friend himself wasn't totally blind when he first went to the Seeing Eye. Even though he still had some slight degree of visual acuity, he was by then what is known as legally blind which is when the best corrected visual acuity is 20/200, or a person's visual field is 20 degrees or less. Before the students got their dogs, there were several occasions when he was able to help others who were completely blind to find the steps or get to the dining room. That really frightened him, I've heard him say, because he realized that it was likely that it would soon be the same for him.

Yet at the same time, he has said that he feels fortunate because he believes he has generally good orientation within his surroundings which makes mobility easier for him than for some. As he got to know the various students that he would be working with, he had some interesting discussions about blindness; and it was reassuring to be able to share some of his own thoughts and feelings among people who could understand because of their own experiences.

Sometimes I try to imagine what it must be like to be blind. I close my eyes and try to experience the world around me without being able to see anything. I know it's not the same as it is for people who are truly blind, but it does give me some idea of what it must be like. I wouldn't recommend doing this when you're walking down the street; but in safer places, it can tell you a lot. When I think of my friend's life, I know that everything that will take place from around this time on will be what I've experienced for just that few minutes of blackness. It helps me to understand his world.

But even among people who are blind, there are differences in the way they think about life without vision. One story that I've heard him tell is, I think, very interesting and shows what I mean.

"I remember sitting in the lounge one night and a young woman came in and sat next to me. She told me she was from Chicago and that she had been blind since birth.

"And she said to me, 'It must be awful to have had your sight and to lose it.'

"I was amazed at her statement and answered, 'I would think it must be awful to never have had sight because I can still see things in my mind. Someone can tell me about an apple or a maple leaf or describe something as the color red, and I can see it from memory. You have had to conjure these things up from nothing.'"

"Well, that's true," she answered. "But I still have my own images. And I have had to live in this world from the beginning, and I've learned what I needed to know to cope all of my life. For you, you have to take everything you already know and put it aside and figure out how to operate as a blind person; you have to learn enough Braille to get by, you have to learn orientation in the dark. You have to be trained how to work with these guide dogs or with the computers that is out there, how to use the screen readers and scanners. And you have to learn how to interact with other people."

"After our conversation, I thought a lot about who was better off. And I realized that, for me, it was better that I once had sight. I recognized, too, how grateful I was that I didn't know I was going blind until later in life and that I was married and had parented wonderful children without that shadow. I'm glad I had been in sports and in the Marines, and all the other things I'd done. I wouldn't trade any of it. Then I thought: so here I am. But if it could be true that becoming blind after having once been able to see is a negative, how can I ultimately turn it into a positive?"

Other conversations took place across the students' time at The Seeing Eye that were good for all of them. My master learned some tricks about how to deal with blindness that he hadn't quite worked out for himself. The first one was a method for dealing with the difficulty of applying toothpaste to a toothbrush.

"That's easy," one of his fellow students told him, "I squeeze out a dab on my finger and apply that to my teeth before I start brushing."

They also talked about different ways for arranging money for everyday spending. My friend had already worked out that problem by assigning different sections in his wallet for the various paper bills.

Ones and fives got their place in the main section, with the smaller domination folded over the larger. Other bills were tucked into their designated places. Usually Judy helped him with this sorting and storing, but bank tellers were always willing to give him his money in a specific order, too. Other students had worked out varying methods, some of which were quite complicated; but they agreed that his way made a lot of sense.

I would guess that one of the side benefits of the training is the opportunity to talk with others who encounter so many of the same things. But their primary reason for being there was to be trained with their dogs, and they were all excited when it was time to meet the guide that had been selected as the best possible match for them.

With each new class, the staff creates a profile of all of the students based on their strength, size, and even personalities. Every candidate provides this information through questionnaires and physicals. The Seeing Eye then considers the dogs in their kennels that are ready to begin working; the instructors know their dogs well because they've been training them for the past four months. With this combined knowledge, they help create the students' matches based on the dogs' physical qualities as well as their temperaments. Because of their long experience, most of the time the matches The Seeing Eye people make provide the best dog for the student as well as the best master for the dog. For the students, knowing that their dogs had been selected especially for them added to their anticipation as the big moment of introductions neared.

The dog The Seeing Eye had chosen for my friend was Trevor, a beautiful male German Shepherd. That Trevor was a fine specimen of our breed, and he had completed his training and was ready to begin his work just before he turned two years old. Because he was a fairly large dog, he seemed from the start to be just the right choice for his tall, strong master.

Soon after they met, it was time for the new team of two to go to their room where they'd have a chance to get better acquainted. Once there, my buddy removed the leash and followed his new dog around the room to let him get accustomed to the unfamiliar surroundings.

Trevor toured the space with his nose as all dogs do, checking out who had been there before and learning what he might encounter before he could decide to settle in. He circled the small room, gave the closet a couple of good sniffs, and then went into the bathroom. After checking out that room with extra care, this exquisitely trained animal lifted his back leg and, well, you know what he did.

Now let's not forget here that my master was not all that keen on dogs, and he had needed to convince himself that cleaning up after one would be an okay part of the package. What he hadn't foreseen was that he'd be doing that job so soon after his arrival, nor that it would take place inside a building, in fact inside the very room where he'd be taking care of his own hygiene.

But after taking a moment for a big sigh, he coaxed Trevor to him and hooked his leash to the bed. With that accomplished, he went to the bathroom to clean up the little "accident" that had taken place there. By the time he had finished the distasteful job, he had calmed down and decided it was not a good time to act disgruntled. After all, it was only their first day together; and he remembered the good advice that he had gotten from the man who called him before he had left home about petting and getting to know the dog. Yes, this was the time for some quality male bonding, he decided. With renewed optimism, he removed the dog's leash and got down on the floor and started to pet him.

"Well Trevor," he said kindly, "we haven't gotten off to a perfect start, but I believe that life is all about forgiveness and new beginnings. And I really do want us to get along well together."

With that, Trevor stood up and repositioned himself with his nose in the corner and his back parts pointed directly toward his new master.

In spite of this less than auspicious first day, the pair started out the next morning on the busy training schedule that the Seeing Eye had planned for them. The new student learned that every day, supervised by their instructor, they would start with a training run; and that regimen would be repeated in the afternoons. Between those runs there was only time for lunch followed by a grooming session and a short rest period. Each night there were classes that included everything imaginable about the care and training of the dogs. One of the first things they learned was the vocabulary that their dogs already knew from their training.

As their instructor explained, "When you say *left,* your dog knows where that is. They, of course, also know what it means when you say *right.* And one word you'll be using a lot is *forward* which tells your dog to get moving. *Come* and *stay* are words they know just as pet dogs do. That is if those pets have had any training at all," he added with a smile in his voice.

"Always remember, you must communicate with your dogs; they are pretty intuitive, but they aren't mind readers. If you want your dog to sit at rest while you're riding in a car, you have to tell him that. If you're walking along and there's a group of stores, your dog won't know where you want to go. It may surprise you that, even with all the training, they can't read. In a situation like that, they're going to be watching for your body language as well as listening for your commands. In an area where your dog is fairly familiar, like near your home, he's going to know to go down the steps and to the sidewalk; and then he's going to hesitate until you tell him which way to go.

"If there are shops near where you live, your dog will be familiar with them; and if you go to a particular place often and he thinks that's where you're headed, he'll wait for you to tell him what to look for. If he seems to want to go into a particular place where you're not intending to go that day, you need to tell the dog, *straight.* Once you sense you're where you want to go from your own experience of counting the steps or whatever tricks you use for yourself, then tell the dog, *Find the door.* That way, with you two working as a team, he'll get you to where you want to go.

"So you see, your dog does have has some limitations. With the training that each of you receive here, between knowing the commands and what to anticipate, it is also important for you to become oriented to your surroundings. That will be easy in places you know well, like around your homes; but it is a little more difficult when you're in a new area. The dogs are trained to look for doors, to look for ways out of a building; but that won't be enough. In this kind of situation, you'll need to pattern your dog to know the route you want to go. If you're in a place for a few days, the dog will pretty much have it down."

During another class the trainer talked about the nature of dogs and how their makeup affected their relationship with their partners. "All dogs love being part of the pack. That goes back to their instincts for survival in the wild. They know all about some dogs wanting to be alpha dogs or others with less power in the group. Dogs just naturally know how that works; they need and like to know where they fit in. This is one of the instincts that make dogs a good choice for Seeing Eye work. The other instinct that they have is about bonding within the group. It is important for you, the blind partner, to understand these things and take charge by becoming the alpha, so that your dog knows where it belongs in your pack.

"Another instinct that dogs have is that they are goal oriented; they like getting from point A to B and then C and D. They feel success when they effectively get from one place to another. So it's your job to work them through the commands they know to get to the goal. The other thing that these dogs, actually all dogs, like is praise for a job well done. When you say, 'Atta Boy,' or 'Atta Girl,' when your dog reaches your goal, it will make it continue to want to work for you; that's how much the reward means to them. I've heard people say that when their dog gets there, it's time to throw a party. That might be just a little over the top, but reinforcing them with your voice is always a part of what you need to do.

"Some of the dogs' instincts are directly related to their noses. That means they can retrace steps; they remember places through their noses. Of course, that instinct can also get them in trouble. At the same time there's that strong instinct to please; so when they're corrected, and remember that you're not hurting them with that correction just regaining their attention, they'll get back to work. Then you give them that 'Atta Boy,' and you're both back on track."

One of the students, a young woman with a beautiful female yellow lab by her side, raised her hand, and asked, "So what if we make mistakes? Let's say we're at a corner and there's a traffic light. I know now I'm supposed to wait and listen for the parallel traffic to move. But maybe there's not enough traffic for me to know for sure. What if I give my dog the 'forward' command, and I've made a mistake, and the traffic is suddenly in our path?"

"That's an excellent question." the instructor answered. "In a situation like that, your dog won't move. This is called intelligent disobedience. Now don't get hung up on the 'disobedient' part. The important word here is *intelligent*. That's how your dog is trained; she's trained to recognize the movement and the potential danger. I can't emphasize enough to all of you: you and your dog are a team. And sometimes, for both of your safety, that intelligent disobedience will make the critical difference.

"Now I'll be honest with you, The Seeing Eye is currently working on a new challenge that's related to your question, and that's how to train you how to deal with the new hybrid cars because at low speeds they just don't make any noise. That makes it difficult for your teamwork to be as effective as it should be sometimes. It may be that you won't hear that car, so it's especially important that your dog is paying attention. This new car situation is, as I say, a challenge; but I'm certain it's one we're going to overcome. So if your dog is exercising intelligent disobedience, it's important that you not scold her. As far as you're concerned, just remember to trust that your dog knows best."

A young man, with his new dog resting quietly beside him, then added, " I don't know if I'm different from everyone else; but when I applied here, I wasn't sure why we needed to stay so long. I guess I just didn't get it that we had so much to learn. I mean, I never thought much about dogs' instincts or their limitations or a thousand other things I've learned. I don't know where I got the idea, but looking back I must have thought that you'd give me a dog, and off we'd go."

Another participant, a good spirited older woman, added with a laugh, "I don't think you're one bit alone in that. I felt the same way with my first dog. What seemed so funny to me during my first training was how much I needed the instruction, not just my dog. That was my biggest surprise."

After everyone had reacted with a little show of applause, the instructor said, "I think what you both said is right on the mark. Just about everyone reacts much the same way. And as you all seem to have figured out, part of the process is learning what your own limitations are, as well as your dogs. Once you get that, you can start to understand how you work together, as a team, to overcome those limitations."

Another thing the participants learned is that working with a dog requires having both good orientation skills and good independent living skills. Dogs require a lot of care, and someone who is overly dependent on others themselves may have difficulty taking responsibility for another creature. Without the right care and without continuous reinforcement of the dogs' training, they can lose their skills and the right perspective for their part in the relationship. This was brought home to the whole group when it turned out that one of their classmates decided he was not ready to take on a dog, and he left before the training session was finished. They hadn't realized he was having difficulty until the instructor told them that their fellow student had decided to leave, but that the organization hoped he would return once he had sorted out some of the problems he was experiencing.

Even though the professionals at The Seeing Eye try to determine if their incoming students have the right orientation and even the right desire for both the responsibility and the independence, sometimes it doesn't work out. The things that are especially hard to predict are where the applicants are in desire to succeed with a dog and in independent living skills. When people go for their initial training with their first dog, most of them are feeling unsure and a little frightened. Then they need to learn a lot of information, while at the same time they must bond with their dogs. Both their ability and their motivation to continue are tested, and sometimes people make the decision not to finish the training.

My master speaks both sadly and hopefully of several people that he has known during his trainings that left The Seeing Eye without a dog. The good news is that some of them went home and improved their orientation and independent living skills and now have completed the program and are working well with their guide partners.

In addition to their classes, from the first day at the Seeing Eye, the new masters do everything with their dogs, including feeding them, taking them out for park time, and cleaning up after them. You may wonder if my buddy was still apprehensive about taking on these responsibilities. The answer that I've heard him tell is that he still did have a number of concerns in those early days. But he was committed, and he worked hard to learn the commands and how to care for Trevor. He also learned everything he could about how the dogs were trained and how to best utilize what his dog knew along with what he himself was learning.

But during the early days, there was some awkwardness between the pair; and Trevor remained a little too aloof. The bonding that my friend was hoping for just didn't seem to be happening. On two occasions when they were out on runs, Trevor simply stopped moving. He just stood there and refused to budge. The first time it happened, the instructor intervened and got him to go forward again. When he balked another time, the instructor told my master what he needed to do to really get the dog's attention and that it was up to him to show Trevor who was the alpha in their pair. This correction might have seemed a little harsh to an outside observer, but the instructor assured his student that it was necessary and that it would work. And it did. That kind of correction was almost never necessary again. My guess is that initially Trevor was trying to determine who in this pair was the master, and the wisdom of the instructor helped to clear up that little confusion.

But even in those slightly shaky early days, there were moments of humor as the two continued their work together. Part of the students' training is going to a grocery store where they learn how to follow a cart and how to negotiate the aisles. After a couple of rounds of this training with their dogs, the students then go back into the store without their instructor to make a purchase. Trevor's master was anticipating this basic skill that he knew he needed, and he was determined for them to do it well on their first try. Once they had successfully made their way through the store and located what they wanted to buy, it was time to make their way back to the counter to check out.

Using his newly learned command, he said, "Hop up, hop up to the counter." And Trevor did a fine job, for in no time, there they were as he had directed.

Then my friend heard a young man ask, "What can I do for you, sir?"

Feeling good about how things were going, he answered with the confident response that he was ready to pay.

"I'd be happy to help you," was the reply, "but I think it would be better if you moved around to the other side."

What he hadn't realized was that his dog had decided to take him *behind* the counter on the cash register side. Fortunately, the people who work in the shops and businesses of Morristown are accustomed to interacting with the students from the neighboring Seeing Eye Organization, so the clerk responded to what had happened with good humor. The pair quickly made their way around to the other side and paid for their purchase. Even with that little glitch, he was thinking that they had done pretty well for their first time shopping as a team.

But then on their way out of the store, the student didn't realize that Trevor, because of his training, thought in terms of his own body plus his master's to determine how much space was needed to clear a narrow path. The newly purchased package was sticking out under my friend's arm, resting on his hip. With this added width, he unfortunately picked off a bottle of wine from the nearby display.

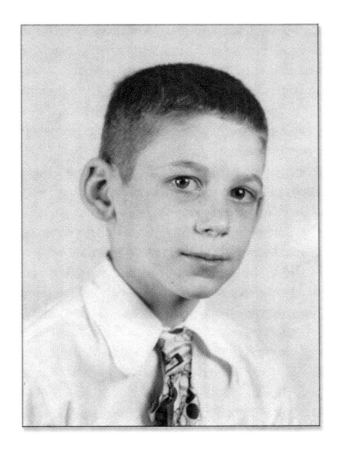

My buddy, all spiffed up for his elementary school picture

Handsome Trevor and his friend enjoy a day at the beach

Beautiful Olive and her new master learning to be a team at The Seeing Eye

A moment of exhilaration in New Hampshire with Ski for Light

Here we are, Judy, my master, and I in our Sunday best

Chapter Ten

*I hold fast to your statutes, O Lord; do not let me be put
to shame. I run in the path of your commands, for you
have set my heart free.   Psalm 119: 31 and 32*

Once they had recovered from this incident on their first
shopping attempt, Trevor and his master kept on working. And then
they finally started to click. The training sessions were going better
each day, and the eager student was open to every possible
opportunity to improve his skills and learn to work in increasing
harmony and confidence with his dog. They grew to know the town of
Morristown together as they walked its friendly streets. It's a
wonderful place for training runs with its combination of a busy town
center and quieter residential areas that lead to the sprawling high
school campus. The wide sidewalks of the shopping area make
maneuvering easy, and the town square provides good practice in its
variety of crossing types.

Toward the end of the training month, their instructor offered the
students the chance to travel to the nearby city of New York; he told
them that the trip would give them a good idea of all they'd learned.
Many of the students who didn't anticipate ever having to go to such a
large and busy place, one where they knew negotiating could be
difficult, declined the offer. But Trevor's master, wanting to try it all,
decided right away that this would be a challenge he'd like to take on.
He also knew that travels for his work and organizations required
visits to large cities; and he thought if he could handle New York, he
could take on anywhere else with greater confidence.

The group traveled by van for the hour-long drive; and happily,
that trip to The Big Apple was an enormous success. Trevor was in
top form, and so was his partner. They maneuvered through all kinds
of tricky situations with a surety and team feeling that had seemed
completely impossible only a couple of weeks before. Their
communications were sharpened as they negotiated the challenges of

the crowded, noisy city streets; they even safely accomplished a ride on an escalator. All in all the bonding that my friend had hoped for had begun, and the apprehensions and concerns he had felt from the beginning of his research into guide dogs were finally put to rest. He now began to truly understand the freedom and independence that he could experience by moving through the world with Trevor, his Seeing Eye Dog.

That night when they returned to the campus, the adventurers met in the lounge with the rest of the group that was curious to hear how things had gone. When it came time for my friend to talk, he relayed a couple of funny stories.

As he tells it, the first went like this: "We had separated for a few minutes because two groups of us were working with one trainer, and Trevor and I were waiting for the others to catch up with us at a street corner. Trevor was sitting patiently as I told him to, when suddenly we heard a voice say, 'Hey mister, the light changed. It's okay now for you to go across.' I thanked him and explained that we were waiting for friends. After a couple of minutes, the others did appear and the instructor said she'd be back as soon as the first team had crossed at the light. As they walked away, I heard that same voice again say, 'Hey mister, they've gone off and left you. Now, what are you going to do?'"

Everyone laughed at this story with appreciation before my friend continued, "Now, a story I think you'll really like also happened today. Trevor and I were walking along, doing great, and again I heard a voice, a different one this time; and I have to admit I didn't like the sound of it. This guy came up and said in what I felt was a threatening tone, 'Hey man, you have a nice dog. Does he bite?' And, as we kept on moving, I answered in my deepest voice, 'Only on my command.'"

That story was received with even louder laughter.

Once the group had enjoyed hearing everyone's tales, they went ahead to their rooms for the night. It had been a good evening, and they were all feeling a little nostalgic about the fact that their time together was coming to a close.

After he had taken Trevor out for park time and gotten them both settled in for the night, he found he couldn't go to sleep. The day had been exciting in so many ways, and he enjoyed remembering how very well he and his canine partner had worked together. One thought lead to another as it sometimes does late at night, and he suddenly felt he understood the truth that The Seeing Eye repeats so often: the key to the whole relationship is to trust your dog. Then he laughed to himself as he realized that the crazy thing was that the dog trusted him.

"I'm the blind person," he thought, "but the dog doesn't know that; all he knows is that he wants to be with me. He wants to do what he's been trained to do. If only my relationships with people could be so dedicated and committed and focused and true as this relationship is becoming. If only my love for everyone around me could be that true."

Then for perhaps the first time, he had the thought which has since that moment been with him every day: "The wonderful thing is that having a guide dog shows and reminds me of God's great love for us because God's love is true; it never falters, it never fails, it is always forgiving. Now that Trevor and I know better how to work together when he and I are out on a walk and he makes a mistake, he always forgives me if I have to correct him. And he always forgives me if I make a mistake, which unfortunately can happen, too.

"The dog doesn't even recognize it as a mistake. And that, he thought, is exactly how God is with us. He doesn't see us as making a mistake; once we have that relationship with Him, he sees us only as His, and He chooses not to see our faults. Wouldn't it be wonderful if in our relationships with each other, we chose not to see each other's faults? Wouldn't it be a wonderful world, and perhaps then it would be exactly as He had hoped from the very beginning."

That night he began to see and think about the parallel of a person's mutual love with a Seeing Eye dog and the love that humans have with their God; for as the dog has a master, that master has an ever-greater Master. And he also realized that, though he was a man who had known many struggles through his life, using a Seeing Eye dog had helped him to learn more about trust and faith because he truly believed God had given him this gift.

He was struck by the realization that the adventure of his relationship with his dog and the adventure of his journey through this life with God beside him created a unique parallel for him. He had gone to Morristown and The Seeing Eye for training and a dog, yet he had not anticipated that the experience would be one in which his faith would be strengthened. The wonder of this realization would stay with him long beyond that night.

When the final day of training arrived, all the students were feeling ready and anxious to try out their new skills at home. My friend, for sure, was anticipating being at home with Judy and eager to return to his job. He was feeling so good about all that had occurred during the past month, and now it was time to put what he and Trevor had learned into practice in their everyday life.

As they gathered together for the last class, one of the instructors praised the students for their hard work and reminded them that, in the event they needed help, The Seeing Eye would be there to provide it. Speaking about the time they had all been together, he said, "Some of you, like others before you, have asked why we spend so much time in training; and my response is that if these dogs were automatic robots, we'd just mail them out."

Knowing the value of what they'd experienced, they all laughed at this observation. They knew without a doubt that their dogs were far from being robots; and they also now knew that they had needed instruction every bit as much as their dogs.

Then the instructor continued, "Now I know how much you're learning to like your dogs, and we certainly want you to enjoy the relationship; but at the same time we don't want you to get the idea that they're perfect. Yes, you know that they've received excellent training; in fact, I like to think it's the best in the world. But for all of that, for each and everyone one of you, your dog is still a dog. Each one has a dog's needs and desires. No matter how well trained they are, they still have their canine instincts.

"This means that when they're working with you, as much as they love you, and I believe that they do, and as much as you are bonded together, as much as you must trust each other, there will be situations where their natural instincts will kick in. I believe that you're going to find that they handle them pretty well; for example, if a cat crosses in front of your path, it's not that they don't see the cat and they will probably even watch it. But when they're in harness, they're trained not to break their stride. They've got a job to do, and they know it's just a cat. That will be the same for most animals that you might encounter.

"Being dogs, there are some things they do very well. They like to work, they like to please you, their masters; and they can see especially well peripherally so they're always tuned in to movement all around. That's what makes them so good at corners because they can see cars coming from one side or the other. That's also helpful if things are coming at you in the middle of a block; they don't have to turn their heads all that far to see what's coming from behind. They don't see things quite the same as humans; we don't think they see all the colors, for example. But what they really see is movement; within forty or fifty feet, they see movement pretty well.

"However, there are some things they don't understand; they have no way to judge how fast a car is coming. That means that it would be prudent for you to cross streets that have a higher traffic speed at a place where traffic is forced to slow up. That's why it's better to cross at a traffic light than at another intersection where traffic doesn't need to stop. They're trained to stop at any crossing; and it's at that point that you become part of the decision process. You've been trained so that when you hear the traffic that's parallel to you, you begin to move when the other traffic that's perpendicular to you stops. That's when you give the forward command because you know you can cross safely where the traffic is stopped. And when one of those cars takes a right or left turn into your intended path, that's where your dog's training kicks in. You may hear the car, but you may not realize where it is. But with your dog's great 270-degree vision, it's going to pick up on that movement and stop until the car has gone by.

"You and your dog are a unit, a team, working together to accomplish the same goals safely, getting you to your destination. There are other types of crossings. It might be what we call a T intersection, and depending on which way you want to cross, you only have to listen to the traffic coming in from the right or left and then cross if there is no traffic there; but your dog will still be looking for cars that might be turning from the top of the T. So in this case, the dog stops, you listen for the traffic that's coming, and then give the forward command when you think it's safe to cross. Once you start walking, if someone turns into your path, that's when the other half of the team, your dog, will make the decision to stop."

After their instructor had given them a few more reminders and they had finished their final class, it was time for the graduates to begin their journeys home. My friend's instructor drove him and Trevor for that all-important trip. He wanted to work with them awhile more that day in their real world as they established the pattern for getting to work. Trevor was extremely conscientious, focused, and serious. His strong alpha personality still required discipline, so that he would always know who was really the master. The trainer understood the dog's nature and worked with them again that day, repeating the importance of being firm and giving all commands as well as praise for a job well done with real conviction.

The next weeks were an important time of adjustment as the graduate became more confident in the use of his dog. At the same time, there were also some adjustments going on at home as this new unit became part of the larger group of wife and family.

Although they had been extremely happy to be reunited after that month of living apart, soon the long-married couple started to sense a new, totally unexpected tension growing between them. A few days after he was home, this unease that had been brewing seemed to be increasing when they were walking together, as they had many times before, in a nearby town.

"Left! Left! John, I said left," cried Judy as she emphatically tried to get him to make a left turn.

"I have to go to the corner," he responded with forced patience in his voice. "I have to stop at the corner and then make the left. I know we're going left, just let me do it the *right* way. And when I make my turn, make sure that you are slightly behind me, off my right shoulder," he instructed.

With tears welling in her eyes, Judy tried to position herself and to understand where it was she was supposed to be when at the same time she was trying to help her husband as she had been doing for several years. Up until the time that he had gone to The Seeing Eye, she had increasingly helped him in maneuvering through his world. Now that he had Trevor in his life, she was truly bewildered about where she was supposed to fit in. She, of course, hadn't been involved in the training. She hadn't had the opportunity to learn how to trust that the dog knew what it was doing, and she had no way to completely understand how this new team of two was supposed to work together. There was no way that she could avoid feeling left out of all the decisions and changes that affected her life almost as much as his.

"It's so frustrating and difficult to understand exactly where in the process I belong," said Judy to her friend Alice one day when they met for lunch. "Before he had a Seeing Eye dog, I knew that I had to help him; I had to tell him what was coming up ahead, let him take my arm or my shoulder, and help him negotiate through a reception, or going to dinner, or wherever he needed to be. I sometimes even needed to help him get around in our home. But now he has this new-found partner; and, please don't get me wrong, I'm glad for this new independence for him. He's very proud that he can work together with his dog and negotiate his way by himself to work or uptown or through a crowded room.

"But where does that leave me? Sometimes I see an obstacle and I say, way too soon, 'Watch out!' But then, of course the dog does get him around it. Or there are the overheads that the dog misses. You know, he hits his head, and then he scolds me for even saying anything. Then he says, 'The dog has to learn, and the only way he'll learn is if you will just let things happen to us where I can reinforce the training and teach him what he needs to be doing.'

"So, what do I do?" she asked. "Do I just let him get hurt? Do I have to let him learn the hard way? I guess that's what I must do. I mean, he so much wants to be able to do everything. And I absolutely understand that. But there are times when he wants my help, too. The other day he said to me, 'Sometimes when I need help, you don't give it to me. And when I don't need help, you're saying way too much. It confuses me and it confuses the training with the dog. We've got to work together on this. You've got to come to an understanding of how we're trained and what you need to do.' So I guess I'm supposed to be a mind reader. I don't know all the rules, and I only get to know them after I've done something that he considers wrong."

"I can really see what you're going through," Alice told her. "He's giving you mixed messages which I understand because both of you are new to all this. But I can also see that it must be so frustrating for you."

"Thank you. Thank you for understanding and listening to me," Judy answered.

"You don't need to thank me. Believe me, I can imagine how hard this must be. But I also know that you two will work it out. I mean that."

"I know you're right. But it's all so complicated. There's even the issue with Trevor. You know how I love dogs; and when he sees me, he gets excited because he knows me. He kind of loses his concentration, and he runs for me. That's not right either. But how do I not have a relationship with the dog, too, when he's living in our home?" she asked.

Such were the frustrations between Trevor's master and his wife when he first came home. But finally after Judy's legitimately feeling left out and being told too often that she wasn't doing things right, they sat down together and talked over the problem. They discussed the fact that she had to learn when to let the dog do its job; and, at the same time, he had to learn when to ask her to assist him and how to best do that. As they talked, the two of them then came to the conclusion that there was a piece of training that could be improved by The Seeing Eye and that they might be able to help in the process.

They called the leadership of the organization and shared the problems they were experiencing and what they had been going through as a couple concerning their first guide dog, and The Seeing Eye people listened. Not too long after that, they got a call asking if the two of them and Trevor would be willing to be a part of the production of a video that could be used to help the family at home better understand what to expect and how to interact with the graduate and the dog. Of course they said that they would be happy to participate. My friend was actually very excited by the prospect.

It wasn't long before some people from The Seeing Eye showed up with a professional video team. While their cameras were recording, they filmed the family walking together. From what I've heard, it was kind of funny because those filmmakers were moving around, dabbing at my master's brow if he was sweating; it was just like a real film production. They also interviewed Judy in their home about the adjustments that were required in the transition from having an important relationship with a blind person to then having a relationship with that person and his Seeing Eye dog.

All of what happened worked out well for both of them because, after his initial euphoria that he had this new independence, he realized that some of the responsibility for making that adjustment was considering how the people at home had a new relationship to work through, as well. He had come to understand that he had to keep the dog's proper use and place in perspective, not allowing his bond with his dog to become more important than his relationships with his wife and children and even with his coworkers and friends. Trevor had to become a natural part of how he was now able to negotiate his way on his journey. Once my master recognized that he had been just a little too bull-headed and determined, he made another big step in incorporating Trevor into his overall life.

Judy had learned a great deal, too, as she related to Alice later, "One of the things that I've noticed, not just about me but others, too, is the tendency to want to reach out and grab John at an intersection when a car is coming. Or if he's coming to a driveway and a car is turning in, there is that natural instinct to grab hold of him and stop him, which is not allowing the dog, who is trained to see these things, stop them on their own. But the other thing that I found is that this relationship that the blind person has with his dog is something that he must work through and get into proper perspective.

"This, I've found out, isn't true just for John; we had the opportunity to get together with another graduate who had trained with him when he got Trevor. We met him and his girlfriend and went out to dinner; and the other graduate began to talk about the bond that takes place between the blind person and The Seeing Eye dog and how this feeling was so strong and how it was of such value to him that he felt, and I couldn't believe he said it right in front of her, that his love for the dog and the relationship with the dog were more valued than his relationship with his girlfriend. As he continued to talk this way, I noticed that she began to cry. I completely understood how she must be feeling; after all, we were in their lives first. These dogs are the new beings on the block. Should they be replacing us?

"What John and I had found out is that they should not be and they really aren't replacing anyone, but they should be helping the blind person to interact with everyone around him. I'm glad to say that I think the young man we had dinner with got a better grip on his relationship with his dog and his girlfriend, for they're now married. And he has entered the ministry. I guess maybe, for all the graduates, it's something that they need to work through. Yes, that relationship and the bond between the dog and his master is a special one, but one to be kept within its proper place.

"I've learned that the value of this dog to John has no monetary value that can be placed on it. The change in his life is that significant. I've watched him, and I know what it means to him. But it also means to me that I don't have to worry about him like I used to. Once I got that in perspective, I realized how incredibly well they work together. I don't have to stay here at home and feel worried that he's going to walk uptown and run into a problem. Now he can do all of that without my help because of his special dog."

When I first heard this story, I was struck by a couple of things, especially about the video my master and Judy made for The Seeing Eye. My first thought was that once again they were able to turn a negative, in this case difficult communications about the new dog, into a positive by making that video and helping others through what they themselves were learning. My second thought was having just a little envy for that handsome Trevor when I realized, hey, I could have been a movie star if I had been the first guide dog in the family.

Chapter Eleven

...and to put on the new self, created to be like God in true righteousness and holiness.   Ephesians 4:24

Even as my master and his wife worked through those adjustments in the beginning, all the benefits of having a dog, of being able to go to the store, or a restaurant, or the bank soon became an important part of his everyday life. Once we guide dogs know an area we can pretty easily get our master to where he needs to be. As a unit, we have to work together; there are certain commands and rules that must be followed for us to be able to lead and do the job we're intended to do.   But even when we're in a new area when we're traveling, with a little bit of help from sighted people, we usually can get ourselves oriented to the area and the new places, even in a hotel, in an airport, or at a conference.

Although some people are surprised by this fact, usually within just a few hours of concentration and patterning we really do know how to get to the places we need to be. So it was soon apparent to my master that the grooming, the playing, and the requiring obedience of the dog on a regular basis were easier than he had anticipated. Although he recognized that some blind people decide they don't want to take on those responsibilities, he honestly believed that for him those chores were worth the effort to gain the independence, the dignity, and the relationship development that he was enjoying. Once those things were firmly established, he became absolutely convinced that he had made the right decision. At The Seeing Eye their slogan is *Independence with Dignity,* and the truth of that phrase was proven to him every day.

He also soon learned that being part of the sighted world with a guide dog caused some highly interesting situations. It wasn't long before he realized how much attention they attracted when they were working together. He also found out that many of the people he encountered in his everyday life, as well as during his travels, simply didn't understand the function of a working dog. Some people seemed to see his guide as a pet rather than the highly trained creatures that we are. We might look just the same as all the other dogs that live with people; but, when we're working, we're not intended to be pets. A number of different events happened in those early months that really drove home for him how often people misunderstand the relationship. I've heard him tell this particular story that I think shows what I mean.

"I remember one time when I was flying into a major airport, we came off the plane and we were headed toward the baggage area to pick up our luggage, and Trevor was being distracted; I mean, he was distracted by everything. I gave him a few corrections verbally, but he kept pulling to go off to the left. Now, I didn't know if someone was talking to him or not, and it could be that someone was trying to get his attention; whatever it was the behavior was causing a real problem.

"Knowing I had to get him back on track, I dropped the handle and gave him a quick leash correction, which is when you drop the handle, pull back on the leash very quickly using a particular command, and correct the dog to bring its attention back to its work. As soon as I had performed this needed discipline, a total stranger, who also happened to be in the airport, started to berate me for mistreating my dog. Well, of course, I knew I wasn't mistreating Trevor but was simply trying to get him to remain focused on his job. What was interesting was there was another individual who came up and quickly scolded the first person for getting in the way. These things do happen."

Like all people who use a guide dog my master has run into many situations where other people want to talk to the dog and even pet him; you know, treat him just like a pet. This kind of thing has happened with me as well as with the other dogs that came before me in my friend's life. Now I've got to be honest here and tell you that I like the attention. I like having people notice me and pet me and praise me. But I also have to be completely truthful and tell you that it's not so easy to stay on task when this kind of pleasant distraction happens. So I thought I'd mention here that if you see a blind person with a guide dog, and they're holding the handle of the harness and the dog is working, please do not look at the dog, please don't try to pet him. If you see the dog and he's at rest and the blind person is not using the harness, if you want to talk to the blind person, do that, but don't talk to the dog. If you have an uncontrollable urge to pet him, always ask his owner if that would be okay. It makes it much easier for us to behave well and do what we're trained to do when people realize that we're on duty.

Another problem that arises concerns food. I almost don't want to tell you this part because I do love my treats, but in good conscience I guess it's necessary. Students are taught at The Seeing Eye all about their dogs' nutritional needs and how to feed us to keep us in top form. Our diet and feeding schedule supply everything we need, and they're designed to keep us healthy and not let us get overweight, which would make it harder to work. Some very well meaning people want to feed us, but unfortunately that can be a big mistake. We are trained to go into restaurants and to social gatherings where food is likely to be abundant. Being dogs we will be tempted by food that's placed right in front of our noses; and if somebody decides to feed us something, in spite of our training, we're happy to take what's offered. But this, of course, should not be done and it can actually result in some real problems for both our masters and us.

I know there have been times when I've been fed by a kindly person who didn't know better, or I've had the opportunity to help myself to people food that has fallen on the floor; and I'm a little embarrassed to admit it, but such occasions have too often resulted in my becoming sick that night or the next morning. It's very important to remember that we dogs are on a very strict routine, both of the day, and also the regular routine of our diets. For us to continue to be successful in negotiating restaurants and socials situations, it's better not to interfere in our work and particularly not to feed us as much as we might enjoy it at the moment. Sigh. Some things you wish you just didn't have to tell.

Even though having a guide dog created some challenging circumstances for my friend in a world of sighted people, the opposite effect also became very obvious. You may remember when I told you about when he first got his cane and finally used it and how he felt that the cane was actually off putting to others, almost a barrier to development of relationships. Remember how he felt when he was standing in the corner at social events, just my master and his darned cane? He soon found out that having a dog had exactly the opposite effect and that it provided lots of opportunities to meet people. In truth, having a dog is an icebreaker; it just seems that the dog is a magnet that draws people in. Even though, if you can believe it, not everybody is a dog lover, even those who are not seem to be drawn in by the wonder of, "How does that dog do that; isn't that incredible."

From the time he first brought Trevor into his life and with all of us since then, when he goes to receptions before dinners and other social events, people are drawn to him rather than seeming uncomfortable with the blind man with the cane as they once were. Often people are waiting, not in line of course, but waiting to come over to talk to him to learn about the dog and all the ways he works on his behalf. Sometimes they may just be waiting to have a chance to say hello to the dog. Either way, he has the opportunity to meet more people; and when he's with his dog, he never feels abandoned in the corner. More often than not people ask many questions about the training and the relationship with the dog. So many people we know love to hear my master's stories about times he's had with his canine buddies. Recently at a social at church someone was asking him about us, and he told this story that is one of my personal favorites.

He started out with a line that I just love: "Guide dogs are amazing." Then he continued, "I remember when Trevor, my first Seeing Eye dog, and I were on a trip to Phoenix, Arizona where I was attending a conference. We had to get from the hotel, down one block, across a street at a traffic light, up several steps past a fountain, and make several rights and lefts in order to get to the building where the workshops were being held. With Judy's help, we patterned Trevor by taking this trip two times and returning back to the hotel room.

"The next day, confident that the dog knew the route, I set out on my own; and we were able to successfully navigate to the right building to attend the workshops. This also was the case on day two. On day three we again made it to the right place in fine shape, and after the meetings I left the building ready to do our normal route back to the hotel room. I must admit I was daydreaming and didn't pay attention to all of the turns; all I knew was that when I got back to the fountain it should have been on my left and that just beyond that would be the steps down to the street, across the traffic light to the hotel.

"But when I arrived at the fountain, I could tell by the sounds that it was now on my right. I was at first perplexed by this, but fortunately there were some other people there; and I asked them if just ahead of the fountain were the steps down to the street to the traffic light and the hotel on the other side. They told me, 'Oh yes, you're right where you want to be.' I couldn't figure out how the dog had apparently gotten me back to the same place but with the fountain on the wrong side. What I found out later was that during the course of my attending the workshops that day, they were shooting some sort of television commercial along what would have been our typical route, the one Judy and I had patterned the dog to follow. We couldn't go that way because things were barricaded while they were in the process of doing the commercial. But the dog knew where, in this case, home was and figured out on his own how to get me back to the hotel by way of the fountain, just on the other side of it. These guide dogs truly do amaze me."

Now I have to tell you that I think that Trevor must have been a pretty smart guy, and he had a great memory for places; his work ethic and ability to get where they needed to go set a high standard for all of us guide dogs. I think another story I've heard about him shows what I mean about his memory. My friend's family always goes to stay at the same house for a couple of weeks of vacation in the summer at a nice town at the seashore called Ocean City. When he would go there with Trevor, the pair would go out for long walks; and Trevor always knew the way to get back to the house. One time, off-season, they went to the same ocean town but stayed in a different place that was several blocks away from their usual summerhouse.

On this visit Trevor and his partner again went out for a walk. When it was time to return, his master completely trusted his guide to get them back to where they were staying. He was right in this trust because Trevor confidently led him along and proudly got them home. The only problem was that Trevor, even after months of not being there, led his partner to their summerhouse, not to the place where they were staying on that particular visit. It didn't take them too long to make their way back to where they should have been, and his friend thought it was pretty funny. But he was also amazed at Trevor's memory and his instincts for getting around.

Actually, it wasn't too long after he had gotten his dog that he became absolutely enchanted by this new relationship. He was so enthusiastic about everything he discovered while working with his canine buddy, that his family started calling him a dog snob. I guess by that they meant that he was acting like a real authority, which seemed a little funny to them since he had never shown any interest in dogs before. But he was really starting to feel like an expert; and though he didn't want to be thought of as a snob about it, The Seeing Eye teaches its students to do it right and that is what he was working to do. He tried to take the knowledge from each of the classes and the training that he'd received and apply it with Trevor on a daily basis.

I have heard him say that, "My Seeing Eye dogs have shed light into my life, which reminds me of the spiritual journey, as well, in that if I am diligent and obey and maintain the good things that I should be maintaining in The Scriptures, God sheds His Light on me every day. It's interesting that spiritually when I get it wrong there is correction and forgiveness and a going forward; and if I make mistakes with the dog, I am reminded very quickly of the same thing because then he doesn't do the job that I know he's trained to do. When one of my children said that I'd become the dog snob, I hadn't even realized I was giving that impression. So I was reminded of the fact that I can't have this relationship with my dog to the detriment of others, especially those who are closest to me."

All of this talk of adjustment might make you wonder how things were going in my master's job. Once he went everywhere with his guide dog, any questions people might have had about his vision were made clear. I heard a friend ask him about this very thing, and this is what he had to say, "One of my colleagues in business shared a conversation he had with someone at a conference or meeting who didn't know me, and they were talking about my being the president of the company. He told me that he had also said to this other man, 'And, oh by the way, he's blind.'

"The second man said, with honest, absolute shock, 'He's what?'

"He was amazed that someone could be blind and the president of a company. My friend, in relaying this story to me, said that he was surprised by his own reaction to the conversation because he never thought of me as being blind. Isn't that funny? You know what I've told people? My guide dog loves me and he loves to work, but he has no clue that I'm blind. But what does that conversation mean? Perhaps my colleague never thought of my blindness because I've always tried to do whatever I was to do to the best of my ability. I've always tried to do what was right in the end.

"So here's this friend saying to me, 'But you don't act blind.' My children have said the same thing. And I say, 'What does that mean? How does a blind person act?' Perhaps it's because, with the help of those around me, I just keep walking forward, never saying 'I can't do that because I'm blind,' but saying 'How can I do that?' There must be a way for me to accomplish the same tasks that a sighted person can accomplish. Of course there are limits; but, in most cases, how do I find a way to get it done? Throughout everything, I've always asked how can I make and keep both confidence and hope reclaimable."

So with an ever-greater acceptance of his condition and an increased understanding of the role of the dog in his world and in that of his family, life continued. In his day-to-day activities my master learned to rely on Trevor to give him an independence of moving about in the world that he had been increasingly losing before his trip to The Seeing Eye. On his trips for work and for vacation travel, Trevor made difficult negotiating possible. Also, in the course of using a guide dog, sometimes he runs into some very humorous situations; and this, I think, is a great story that my master loves to tell and one that always makes his listeners laugh.

"There was a time when Judy and I were flying from Springfield, Missouri to St Louis where we were to pick up a connecting flight to Philadelphia. Unfortunately there were some severe thunderstorms in the area that night; and we were delayed in Springfield, and that made us late getting to St Louis, which meant we missed our connecting flight. Now, of course I have to take care of the dog's needs no matter what else might be happening. Generally I try to arrange flights so that I don't have to take the dog outside; but in this case because our timing was so messed up with delays, we were forced, while making arrangements for a new flight to Philadelphia, to have to get the dog outside of the airport to relieve himself.

"We proceeded to find the front door, and I was about five paces in front of Judy. She came through the door behind me where she saw a young man standing outside. I had gone ahead, but she stopped and turned and asked him very politely, 'Can you please tell me where we can find some grass?'

"Well, as soon as she said it and he started to speak, I knew that this stranger must be hearing it all wrong.

"Stammering and stuttering he could only say, 'I, well I, uh...'

"It was obvious to me that he was having a hard time connecting this request to the attractive and conservatively dressed woman who stood smiling pleasantly in front of him. I wouldn't be surprised if she made him think, with some horror, of his own mother asking the same thing.

"I turned quickly with the dog, trying to get back to Judy; when, as the young man continued stuttering, she added quite sweetly, 'We don't need much, we just need a little.'

"Well, of course, that made it all the worse, and his total misunderstanding of her questions, not knowing that she was with my dog and me, was becoming very comical to me.

"I finally got back to them and explained, 'Excuse me, but we're looking for a place where there's some grass where the dog might relieve himself.' The young man was at that point visibly relieved to understand what she had actually been requesting."

Chapter Twelve

Never doubt in the dark what God has told you in the light.
Victor Edward Raymond

The next few years passed quickly and happily for my master and his family and Trevor, too. The children were now established in their adult lives, and they were all living near enough to their parents for them to continue to be a very close group. My friend's career was thriving, and his company was expanding and steadily becoming of increasing importance in their area. Trevor had become something of a celebrity in the town. His picture was frequently seen in the local newspaper, and he even had a place of honor on the company webpage.

My master's work and involvement in a variety of organizations required quite a bit of travel; and because he now had Trevor, he felt confident to go anywhere. As I mentioned before, that fine boy attracted a great deal of positive attention. We guide dogs really do appeal to all kinds of people; and, well to be honest, we can be a magnet for women. They really seem to love us. For some reason, they seem to think we're cute. My master often relays an experience that helps to illustrate my point.

"One time we were traveling out of Atlanta by plane. Judy and I had been able to get bulkhead seats, which we normally try to do because there is a little more foot room for the dog to be able to lie on the floor. If we're lucky enough to get all three seats when there's not a full plane, oftentimes she'll sit in the window seat, we'll leave the middle one open, and I'll sit on the aisle. That was the case on this particular flight. We had boarded and we were comfortably seated in the plane, and Trevor was settled on the floor in front of me.

"One of the stewardesses came over, knelt down, and was talking to the dog, asking me questions about him, and just basically ohhing and ahhing. Then a second stewardess came up and she knelt down, too, balancing herself with her hand placed on my knee. She also was admiring Trevor and asking questions about him. A third stewardess joined us and kind of perched on the arm of my seat. All three of them were fussing over the dog. Then they told me that if there was anything they could do, to please let them know.

"When it was time for them to get back to work and they left, Judy reached across the empty middle seat and suggested that maybe we should hold hands. That's when I made perhaps one of the major mistakes in my life, and said, 'I'm sorry, but do I know you?'"

Fortunately that good woman gave him a little smack on the hand and took his comment lightheartedly; after all their years of being together, she knew his sense of humor well. Trevor, of course, wasn't overly impressed with any of what had happened; and he decided that, once the plane was in the air, he was mostly off duty. He stretched himself out with a sigh and enjoyed the rest of the flight.

All of us guide dogs have distinctive personalities, and Trevor's included his being especially conscientious and serious about his work. Yes, our training is the same, but each of us retains our basic nature. Now, as you probably have gathered, although I am Patton, The General, I don't have the personality of my namesake. Actually, I'm described as pretty easy-going, mild mannered, and laid back. I understand that Trevor was a terrific guide dog and a role model for all of us; yet as I mentioned earlier, he also had an alpha, wanting-to-be-in-charge attitude from time to time. You'll remember how my master talked about having to take control during their first days together. Once that issue was resolved, Trevor gave him several years of truly devoted service, and his loyalty was absolute. But then some troubles started to happen. It seems that there came to be times when that loyal dog thought he knew what was best, even when he sometimes misjudged a situation.

There was a period of time when Trevor's life included a great deal of travel for both business and vacations. They flew to Arizona in September; and before the month was out, they then traveled to Banff Springs in Canada. Within three months, they flew again, this time to Florida for a business meeting. When they returned home from there, they took a trip to Maine. When you think of it, that's pretty much touching the four corners of North America within a short time.

Although we are professional guide dogs and we generally love to travel, that many airplane trips and visits to strange places can be a little overwhelming. I think that travel for us includes a lot of the same stresses that it does for people. There are many tense situations that involve new circumstances for us to have to guide our master around. We have to make decisions about where he might want to go when the territory is just as unfamiliar to us as it is to him. Unlike at home, it isn't always clear when or how we'll be expected to work.

After that series of trips all over the continent, there was a fifth trip for Trevor that year to a place in western Pennsylvania. It was there that his master began to worry about his dog's reactions to the stress of so much travel, which had started manifesting itself in Trevor's taking on a very protective attitude concerning people who came into his master's and Judy's path. One night the three of them were walking through a hotel, and they came to a corner. As they made the turn, they encountered a stranger. Trevor seemed to be startled by this chance meeting of paths, and he snarled at the unsuspecting man. When Judy thought about it later, she realized that there had been something disconcerting to her about the man's expression, and she had reacted with momentary uneasiness. She wondered if Trevor, who was so in tune with both of them, had somehow picked up on her own reaction.

But then, such things continued to happen. There was an evening when they were all in Florida. It was beautiful outside, sometime around sunset; and they decided to walk awhile to enjoy the view and the weather. Again, someone came toward them on their path and Trevor reacted violently. He lunged toward the man, actually hitting him on the chest, before his master could pull him back. Once again Judy recalled feeling just an instant's uncertainty about the stranger before the dog reacted so violently. You can imagine how embarrassed they must have felt.

For whatever unknown reason, Trevor's reactions were the most pronounced when anyone had on a uniform. Waiters in uniform caused him to react with a growl; and on one occasion, a security guard in Florida who was trying to help my master enter the right door also received both a snarl and growl from the now overly protective Trevor. As he started becoming more conscious about his dog's behavior, my master thought back to the flight home from Canada when a pilot had walked by, and said, "We're going to the U.S.A. today." Trevor had reacted to the pilot's uniform and seemed to have decided that all Canadian airplane pilots were now part of a conspiracy against his family and him. At the time it hadn't seemed that important; but after the other incidents had happened, it began to feel like another warning.

When they were at home in between their travels, Trevor was completely himself and behaved as he always had in his normal environment. Although his master was somewhat reassured by his dog's return to good manners and perfect obedience, he couldn't help feeling an underlying concern. He thought that if they were always able to be in a regular routine in familiar surroundings, that all would be well. But travel had become an increasingly necessary part of his life for work; and now that the children were raised, he and Judy wanted to enjoy the freedom of being able to take vacation trips. As he continued to think through what was going on, he decided that maybe Trevor had just needed a break and that he'd be okay. After all, they had been on so many trips in a pretty short time. Unfortunately, his optimism was short-lived.

One of the business organizations that my master belonged to was having a conference in New York City that he needed to attend. Once they got there, they found that they were staying at a very nice hotel, one that had bellhops and doormen, all in uniform. My master was returning from a meeting outside of the hotel, and he was approaching the door when Trevor began to lunge and growl. Unfortunately, this behavior did not give the doorman a great deal of confidence about Trevor's intent. True, his master had him under control, but the frightened man wisely decided to stay on the other side of the door away from the dog.

When they finally got inside the hotel, Trevor's master, wanting to get them quickly to their room, headed directly toward the elevators. Once they got there, a couple of bellhops in uniform were coming through one of the sliding doors. The sight of those men sent poor Trevor into a complete frenzy. His friend had to literally drag a growling, snarling Seeing Eye dog across the hotel lobby while waiting for the bellhops to clear the elevator area so he could get in and get to his room. That traumatic incident made him realize that he had to take Trevor's problem seriously; as much as he had wanted everything to be all right, it had become obvious that it was not simply going to go away. Wonderful, dutiful, hard-working Trevor had taken on a protective role that became an impossible hindrance to his otherwise excellent ability to lead.

Instructors at The Seeing Eye tried working with Trevor to change this negative behavior, but they didn't have success. Every time they exposed him to a person in uniform, he reacted in the same inappropriate way; and there was no explanation for this behavior. Unfortunately, after giving it their best effort, they decided that Trevor's growing security consciousness was not conducive to his being able to continue to work as a guide dog. The instructors reminded my master that each dog has a basic nature that can't be changed regardless of the amount of training. Trevor had been with his partner for several years, and all of what he had done for him was so valuable that he was completely committed to having a dog in his life. But what could he do if even professional trainers weren't able to help his good friend return to what he had once been? After anguishing about how to deal with this unsolvable problem, he finally decided that the best thing for both of them was to take The Seeing Eye's advice and retire his beloved dog.

At first Trevor didn't understand that he would no longer be going everywhere with his master; he would go to the door, ready to be put in his harness and head out to do his job. I've heard Judy say that he used to stand by the door and look out the window next to it, watching his best friend walk away. After that he would generally settle down; but at the end of the day, he seemed to know when it was time for his friend to return. He would go to the door and wait patiently. Devoted Trevor continued this pattern throughout the rest of his life. He would have been ready to get into harness and go to work until his final day.

But even though he continued to go to the door each time his master left, after awhile in most ways he started to enjoy his role in the family as a pet. He spent a lot of time riding shotgun with Judy while she was out on errands. He was, by then, well known about town and he continued to enjoy a great deal of attention. Sometimes when Judy would take a trip to the grocery store, there would be a crossing guard from the elementary school who was stopping for a cup of coffee; and he would sit with Trevor at the back tailgate of the station wagon. He always gave Trevor a biscuit. Being very smart, he was never satisfied with one; and he always knew that with a little gentle persuasion he would get two.

Much later when I came home to begin my service, Trevor was still a highly honored dog in the family. Sadly, by then he had grown old and he was also sick. I lived with him for only a week before he had to be taken to the veterinary hospital where it was discovered that he had stomach cancer. In looking back, my master has wondered if perhaps Trevor had been unwell much longer than they realized at the time and if some of his aggression might have been connected to his failing health.

I remember the profound sadness of both my master and his wife the day that Trevor left this earth. They had been very close to him, for he had worked five and a half years guiding his master and then had spent the remainder of his life as a devoted pet. Yes, it was a sad day; and I made space for my master and his wife to mourn Trevor's leaving. I understood it; I completely understand the bond, the trust, and the love.

But I also learned from them that this world is temporary, that we all have to pass through this life; and that at the end of the day, there is that Big Biscuit. And I'm not talking about a treat to chew on. In my master and Judy's life and for all people, at the end of the day, if they place their trust and love in Jesus Christ, their reward will be an eternity with Him, not because of anything that they did, not because of anything they do, but because of what Jesus did for them on Calvary. I like to think that reward was also waiting for Trevor.

After he had made the tough decision to retire Trevor, my friend returned to The Seeing Eye to get his second dog. As I mentioned before, returning participants in the program require a shorter training session; but it's still necessary to work with an instructor and the new dog at the campus even if they're getting the tenth one. This trip was much easier than the first had been. All of his concerns that had preceded that visit had been completely put to rest, and returning as a veteran of the program had that feeling of familiarity and belonging that most repeat experiences do.

This time my master was matched with a crossbreed between a Golden Retriever and a Yellow Lab named Olive. She had been given that unusual name because she was part of an "O" litter. That Olive was a wonderful little girl. Well, actually she wasn't so little; she was an eighty-five pound dog with an especially pretty face and a magnificent golden coat. From what I've heard, she was, in fact, sturdier and even a little stronger than we German Shepherds usually are. Olive truly was energetic, and she could really move out in harness. She also had a wonderful disposition; she loved everyone and everyone loved her in return.

One of the things that they repeat at The Seeing Eye over and over is Trust Your Dog, and Olive's master was reminded of that a couple of different times when he and his new dog were in training. I heard him talk about this with some friends over dinner not too long ago, and I'll let him tell the story on himself.

"I remember one time in training with Olive we were almost finished with a particular route, and she had done well. Then we came upon another dog that decided to take a little park time next to the sidewalk where there was grass. Olive made a very quick move to go around the other dog; and quite honestly, I thought for some reason that she had gone to the right when she had actually gone to the left. We were on the grass next to the street, while I thought I was on the lawn on the other side of the sidewalk. When we passed the obstacle of the dog, I thought I needed to go back to the left. Initially Olive wanted to go back to the right, but I told her to hop left. We wound up walking out on the street.

"My instructor took some time to make a little good-natured fun of me, and reminded me, once again, to: 'Trust your dog.'

"That is a common theme and one that's necessary to being a good dog handler and a solid graduate of The Seeing Eye. Is it hard to always trust your dog? Sure it is. We human beings want to have control, even when we can't see. And this trust is a learning process. There I was back in training for the second time, and I was still learning about trusting my dog. It would not be the last time that I would need to learn that lesson; unfortunately, there would come a time when that trust was critical. But that's something that I don't even like to think about."

As he was reminiscing about Olive with his friends that night, he went on to tell another story about their training together. "We were out on the routes for one of our runs. In this situation, they set up different kinds of barriers and they always have a dog distraction. They usually set up a big German Shepherd waiting to bark and carry on, and what you're supposed to do is go by with your dog in training, telling the dog, 'Leave it, leave it.' The idea is for the dog to negotiate around any distraction.

"Olive didn't react exactly as she was supposed to with this particular commotion and decided to really get moving. It seemed, quite honestly, as if she had forgotten about me. But I hung on and tried to keep up with her, hoping she knew what she was doing. There I was, following my dog, and she went to the left of one of those newspaper stands that are out on city corners which, of course, I couldn't see as I stormed along after her. I hit that thing full bore, right in the chest. I knocked the newsstand over and scared the living daylight out of Olive. I was fortunate I wasn't hurt and neither was she, but I must admit that I was pretty well stunned."

So I guess you can see that in the early days Olive's only real problem was that constant distractions were part of her effort. She thought nothing of wanting to chase a squirrel, a cat, or a rabbit.

Unfortunately those temptations are all major no no's for us working dogs. I've heard my master say that he was pretty sure that in Olive's mind there was a party taking place around every corner and that she was anxious to get to it. Subduing this overly enthusiastic and happy personality, though, was something that he and Olive had worked on all through training.

Even when he first got Olive home, she really did take a lot of effort; and at first her master worried that maybe The Seeing Eye had made a mistake by pairing them. Although he knew that they worked hard to match dogs and owners, he did have reasons to wonder if she was the right dog for him. He knew that he had to correct her much more often than he had needed to do with Trevor, but at the same time he recognized that she was an extremely sturdy and cheerful dog. It was impossible not to love her buoyant good nature. Of course this good nature would also lead to some interesting incidents and circumstances.

chapter Thirteen

Because of the Lord's great love we are not consumed,
for his compassions never fail.   Lamentations 3:22

Olive and Trevor got along well from the start. He, naturally, continued to be serious and dutiful; but he also tolerated and even seemed to enjoy Olive's antics. She liked to play games with him, and Trevor always took her clowning around in his mature stride. Being very ingenious, she actually seemed to think through ways to get her friend's attention. One of her favorite amusements would take place when he would have a toy that she wanted, if only because he seemed to be enjoying it. She'd watch him for a minute, then she'd run to the front door and make a bit of a fuss as if someone were outside. Trevor, because he was so conscientious, would hurry to the door to see what was going on, only to find that there was no one there. While he was occupied making sure that all was well, Olive would rush back and claim the toy. What can I say? That girl was one clever trickster.

All of this talk about Olive's playful nature makes me think of a story I heard my master tell his friends, The Group, at our café, "One night Judy and I went to the theater, and there was a wine and cheese party outside as part of the evening's events. We were sharing a table with some other people, and Olive was lying at my left side. We were enjoying our refreshments and pretty soon the call came that it was time for the audience to find their seats. I reached down to Olive for her to pay attention and get up, when suddenly I noticed an interesting smell that seemed to be coming from my dog.

"After a second's thought, I recognized it as the smell of strawberries. I reached down and Olive turned toward me; and I felt a sticky, creamy substance all over her face. What I discovered was that she had very quietly wriggled her nose into the purse of one of the women we were sitting with and had extracted a tube of strawberry-flavored lip gloss and had smeared it all over her nose and lips. This smell so permeated Olive and, as a result, me that during the intermission of the show we finally had to leave because it was just a bit much. That was life with Olive, constantly watching her and constantly worrying about her, but all the time enjoying a few laughs with her, too.

"And that reminds me of the time that she stole a bar of soap from our shower. When I went to get it from her, she ingested it quickly. All that I heard was, 'Gulp, gulp.' We both paid a price for the next couple of days with what she was producing from both ends. Ah, my beautiful Olive."

I've heard my friend say that when he would discipline Olive with a leash correction she would react as if to say, "Is that all you got?" She often required a two-handed correction while Trevor had usually only needed a one-handed reminder. She was just a little more oblivious to discipline than he had been. I personally think that tendency only had to do with her energetic mind and belief that it was okay to chase that tantalizing rabbit or cat, but of course it was not okay.

On the positive side, Olive did do well in other settings. She would lie down and stay down when they were at work or in business meetings while traveling, and that was important to her master. He needed to be able to concentrate on his job and not be distracted by his dog. But then there was that little problem when they needed to travel on airplanes.

As he tells it, "Olive did have trouble settling down and sometimes needed some doggie Valium before flights. We started with a half a pill and worked our way up to two whole ones. As I was considering that it might take three, a friend of mine suggested that perhaps it would be better if I took the two pills myself and just forgot it. In any case, she was a high-energy dog."

In spite of these initial challenges, Olive was a hard worker; and as she and her partner continued their efforts together for two years, she kept getting better and better at doing her job. She had needed to overcome the tendency to be distracted, and that was a hard lesson for her. But for all of her early problems, as you will see, she ended up to be a true heroine.

Of all the tales I've heard about Olive my personal favorite took place when my friend and his wife went with another couple on a vacation tour from Vancouver to Banff Springs, Canada on the glass-topped train. In spite of the fact that they were traveling in early May, it snowed the whole time.

"It was a wonderful trip," my buddy remembers, "the scenery that Judy got to see and tell me about was outstanding; she has always said it was one of her favorite, if not her favorite vacation, that we've taken. When we went to meals on the train we were assigned our own booth because of having the dog with us. One morning the snow was coming down as we were served a delicious salmon and poached egg breakfast and a mimosa.

"We were sitting there relaxing, sipping our mimosas, and Judy reached over, took my hand in hers, and said, 'This is the most fantastic trip that we've ever been on; it's a dream come true. I love the train, and the snow is so beautiful as we go across the mountains. It's almost unbelievable everywhere I look.' As I was picturing the landscape that she was describing, I felt just like Dr. Zhivago, taking Lara to the ice palace.

"Now it so happened on that trip that at one point the conductor had to back the train on to a siding while another train came through the tunnel in the Canadian Rockies. So we were at a stop, and we were sitting in our car on the sideline. The next thing that I knew this lady came up; and she, well how can I say it, she was extremely gregarious. I mean to tell you, I wasn't one bit surprised when Judy later described her to me as the epitome of the California girl. Apparently, she was wearing a very tight-fitting spandex outfit that seemed to go with her bright blond hair. She knelt down and was actually kissing Olive; and she, well I don't know how else to put this, but she was lying across my thigh in her spandex outfit. She was fussing with Olive and kissing her on the lips. As you can imagine, my happy girl dog thought that was just fine. But at the same time our visitor was also fussing with me and asking me about the dog.

"Judy was sitting on the seat beside me at the train window. No, actually I guess she was standing at this point; I think she was getting ready to defend the dog though I'm not sure she was so ready to defend me. But this woman was, shall we say, extremely friendly, and Judy finally said, 'I think that you've stimulated them quite enough.'

"Of course, getting the dog stimulated was no problem because she, as I've said, was always looking for the next party. And this out-going girl from California brought out all the best party spirit in her. But I also think Judy was pretty sick and tired of our uninvited visitor's draping herself over her husband's lap. It was interesting that when we got to the resort at Banff Springs, we saw this same gal later downtown, still in spandex, still very outgoing, hailing a cab. She got into the front seat of the cab, sitting right next to the driver, which we in our Eastern ways thought was unusual; but hey, she was from California, right? Maybe things are different there."

So across those couple of years, Olive not only learned how to do her job increasingly well, but she also provided quite a bit of amusement for her master. She was an exceptional dog, and her increasing maturity and determination to do her job well earned her a special place in his heart. Because of first Trevor's and then Olive's devotion to him, he was able to function in the sighted world with a confidence and sense of independence that he had once feared would be impossible. Then an event happened which was to serve as a very real reminder of The Seeing Eye's edict about trust.

Olive began most of her days with a regular routine. Her master would awaken very early, long before it was light outside; and his first thought was to tend to his dogs. After that, he and Olive headed out for their usual early morning walk which was about two or two and a half miles long; this routine was a good way to get in some exercise for both of them before my friend needed to get home for his shower and breakfast and then head out to work.

"I love getting up early, and its going to be a beautiful day," he said to them that morning. "Come on, Olive, let's get you something to eat, but first we need to get you outside. Here we go. Ah Trevor, there you are. How are you doing this morning, Buddy? Okay you beautiful dogs let's go out back. You two go and run a little bit while I get your bowls and prepare your breakfast."

Once he was organized, he called, "Okay, come on in, guys. Hello, Olive, good girl. Good boy, Trevor. Ah yes, the early morning breakfast. You guys eat while I do some of my warm up exercises. Then Olive I'll be back for you, and Trevor can enjoy a little nap."

After they had eaten, he put on Olive's harness and leash and they were ready to go out for their walk. My master had asked an instructor what he thought if he took the dog for a two-mile walk every morning and he answered, "That's a perfect doggie world." So off they went on that October morning. He had awakened so early that it was still dark when they left the house.

As he remembers that day, he says, "Usually Olive and I were pretty focused as we began our walk. We started out from our house at a good pace, crossed at the traffic light, and headed into the neighborhood where my parents once lived. In my late teens, they had moved a little way outside of town; so at one time it had been my home, too. We looped around those streets a couple of times, passing our old house."

They were about a half a mile from the finish where they had to make a difficult crossing on what can be a busy street. However, it was still only a little after five o'clock, and there usually isn't much traffic in our town at that time. My master remembers that by then he had been daydreaming a bit, and that Olive was walking along on automatic pilot.

As they approached what he thought was the intersection that would take them back to their neighborhood, Olive made a move down into a curb ramp; and then he heard a truck from the left which he knew had to be traveling on the main street, the one which he needed to cross to go home. From the sound, it seemed as if it was cresting the top of the hill, which probably meant it was about the length of a football field away. Given the location of the truck based on what he was hearing, they had plenty of time to cross the street before it would pass by in the dim light of the early dawn.

He picked up the pace a little bit, beginning to move at a semi-jog; and they started to cross. Soon he realized they weren't getting to the other side as they should have been, and he thought Olive might be taking them on an angle which would mean they might still be in the middle of the street. My master could hear the truck getting closer and closer, and he knew that it was unlikely that the driver could see them in the dim light. But he and Olive, even though they were moving quickly, still weren't getting to the other side. Feeling his panic rising, he dropped the handle of the harness, just holding the leash, and broke into a full run.

Later he knew that the best thing would have been if he had just stopped and let the dog do what she knew to do. But he didn't. As he tells it, he had let human instinct kick in, as well as his instinct to control. He kept running, and Olive was running with him. Yet they still weren't getting to safety. None of it was making sense to him.

Where was he?

He had lost all sense of orientation and felt surrounded by darkness and frantic confusion. Then he realized that he must be running right toward the front of the truck, directly into its path. As he felt Olive pulling him to the right, he could hear the sound of brakes and hoped that the driver had finally seen them. But then he heard the brakes lock up, and he knew how close the danger must be. In that instant he realized with horror that it was too late. The truck couldn't possibly stop in time, and they were going to be hit.

The thought that sped through his mind at that moment was, "Oh no, this is how I'm leaving this world. And everyone will blame the dog, but it's not her fault."

He remembers that, "The truck bore down on us with the terrible shriek of its brakes and tires. At the last second, Olive, shielding me with her body, pushed me farther to the right and almost got us clear of the truck's path. But unfortunately, as hard as she had tried, Olive and I were both struck by the left fender of the dump truck. As I felt myself being lifted off my feet and thrown on my back, I released the leash. After I crashed to the ground, I lay there hyperventilating and soon realized I had no idea where Olive had gone. I reached frantically around me trying to find her.

"The driver jumped out of his truck yelling, 'You ran right out in front of me. Man, you were right in front of me. I never saw you until the last second.'

"'I know. I know that's what happened," I told him as I gasped for air.

"As I got myself up on my feet, I felt a great deal of concern for the driver and the shock he had to be going through. But my most urgent thought was, 'Where is Olive?'

"I apologized to the driver telling him again it wasn't his fault.

"'I made a mistake, I panicked. But where is my dog? She's my Seeing Eye dog, and she was trying to help me. I let go of her leash, and I don't feel her here where I fell. Can you see her? Can you see where she's gone?'

"The driver let me put my hand on his shoulder and walked me back up the street to where Olive was sitting, ironically I realized even then, on the front yard of what had once been my parents' house.

"'Olive, come,' I called to her.

"She answered me with a whimper. She was obviously terrified and disoriented.

"'Olive, it's okay. Come honey.' She slowly crawled over to me, and I grabbed her by the head and held her close. I felt the harness handle, and it was slightly bent so I knew she must have been hit.

"'Can you tell is she hurt anywhere? Is she bleeding, is she okay? Is she limping?' I asked the driver as I worked my hands carefully over her shaking body.

"'I don't see anything,' he told me.

"As I held Olive close to me, the truck driver and I exchanged names and numbers. After he helped us make our way across the street, she and I began to slowly walk the half-mile back to our house. Though physically I thought I was all right, emotionally I was in complete turmoil. I couldn't imagine what I could tell Judy, how I could explain what had happened without unnecessarily alarming her. And then there was the remorse of having made a mistake that could have resulted in a much worse outcome. I tried to calm myself with the fact that I was alive; I was alive and conscious and in one piece.

Though Olive was walking much slower than her usual pace, I thought that was understandable after what she had been through; and the driver had reassured me that she had no visible injuries.

"But then, as we entered the front door and I bent over to take off her harness, I smelled blood and discovered that her back end was wet. Running my hand around her hindquarters and tail, I came to the horrified realization that she must be seriously injured. I could feel that she was bleeding severely. I called for Judy to come down from upstairs where she was just awakening, and we tried to clean Olive to determine where she was hurt. As we washed away the blood, we realized that she had an abrasion along her side; and with even more dread, we discovered that her tail was all but severed. We wrapped her in clean towels and rushed to the veterinary clinic where they immediately prepared her for emergency surgery. Believing that she was getting the best possible care, Judy then insisted that we go home and check to see if I was injured as well.

"When we got there, I think I was probably in shock. It was partly the awareness that I was still living. In those last instants before impact, I had felt so sure that my life would end that morning. At the same time, I was feeling terrible about not trusting my dog. When I showered, I realized that I, too, had cuts and bruises on my left side. But, over Judy's protests, I went to work because I had an important meeting scheduled that I didn't feel I could miss.

"After that appointment, when it became known to my staff that I had been in an accident with my dog, they along with Judy convinced me that I needed to get to the emergency room. As it turned out, my injuries were minor. We got Olive home after her surgery, and I will always remember the feelings of guilt I had about putting my dog and myself in harm's way because I hadn't followed the rules."

Much to his very deep regret, my dear friend had forgotten Rule Number One: Trust Your Dog. From what he says, there is no question in his mind that if he had just stopped and let Olive do her work, what happened on that early morning walk would not have occurred. For as he panicked and ran, holding the leash, they had actually been running up the street when he had thought they were crossing. Later he understood that, in reality, they had been forty feet away from the intersection where he had meant to cross; and he should have waited for the truck to pass by.

Chapter Fourteen

Delight yourself in the Lord and he will give you the desires of your heart. Psalm 37:4

The good news is that, because of Olive's valiant effort, neither of them was hurt nearly as severely as they could have been. But unfortunately, Olive did eventually need surgery. Although the vet had tried just bandaging the wound in the hopes that it would heal, it became necessary to remove part of her tail. After she completely recovered, my master tried to take her back into the working mode. The first day she actually did quite well, and he was hopeful that she was going to be all right. On the second day, as they were walking down the street to the office, there was a truck coming along behind them. When Olive heard that truck, she panicked. It was then that he realized they had a serious problem.

That afternoon an instructor picked Olive up and took her back to The Seeing Eye where they tried for four weeks to help her overcome her fears. But she wanted nothing to do with being near traffic anymore, and even the experts couldn't get her past her terror enough for her to be able to serve as a guide dog again. The trainers explained to her master that in Olive's mind the accident had been the ultimate correction. Because she misunderstood what had actually happened, she thought that she'd been punished.

Since it was impossible for her to work, they were forced to make the decision to retire her. That was a sad time. That was a sad time particularly for my friend because he knew that he had broken Rule One. Seeing Eye dogs are highly trained; and although we can make mistakes, we are taught to do our job. Perhaps Olive's exuberance and tendency to being distracted somewhat led her partner to think that he couldn't trust her completely. But looking back on what happened, he's certain that had he trusted her, it would have been the best choice. He learned a very hard lesson.

That distressing incident with Olive, as serious things often do, raised questions for my master that extended even beyond his feelings about what had happened on that morning. I know how much impact it must have had on him because I've heard him talk about it in a very serious way. Usually he has a great sense of humor, and he loves to laugh and make others laugh as well. In almost every situation, he's able to find some way to add a little lightness to a story. But I recently heard him talking with his friend Chuck about trust, and there were no little jokes or funny stories in what he had to say. First he was talking about Olive, and then his thoughts went on to other things that were on his mind.

"The importance of practicing and maintaining the discipline that you learn, whether it is from Scripture or The Seeing Eye, was brought home very vividly to me when I was working with Olive. I think God has protected me all of my life, and I know for sure that He did that day. I made a terrible mistake that morning. I have also done things in my life that have unintentionally but selfishly hurt people, hopefully not too badly; but these things have led to my having to make decisions to lay this or that down…and to go on.

"Through all of these mistakes I have had to draw out of the negative the idea that there is a positive and to grab hold of that positive to go forward. Many times these mistakes involved my ability to trust. I think in my career, as I lost my vision, I was forced to be dependent on other people, first for rides, but also for getting certain parts of the job done, which meant that I had to be able to delegate and that required trust. Now, I won't kid you: I would have much rather done everything myself and controlled the situation. But I think part of any success that I had as a leader was the fact that I was forced to delegate and to trust, and I always believed that helped others grow. "Trust is an amazing thing. We all want to trust, and yet there are times that we fail each other. I've found that the one and true thing that I can trust absolutely is God and His gift of full pardon and forgiveness through Jesus Christ. To be honest with you, I don't know where I would be without God. And yet I see that in our relationships with each other we sometimes withhold that same grace of forgiveness that God gives through His Son so freely."

"I know what you mean," Chuck said. "There are people who have hurt me, people that have turned against me, or people that I should just forgive. And I struggle to forgive them. At the same time, I also know that some of them struggle to forgive me. I guess in relationships we can be limited. We may say to someone that we forgive him, but do we always really forget? God is not like that. He said, 'I love you so much I am going to send my Son to the earth. He is going to take your place and take on that which you deserve; and if you accept that, then I will choose to forget because it is a debt that has already been paid.'"

My friend smiled, then said, "It would be like a representative of a bank calling you up on the phone one day and saying, 'We know that you owe us a hundred thousand dollars, but we've chosen to forgive you and to forget your debt.' Now wouldn't that be amazing? Wouldn't we be a grateful people? That's what's been done for us by God through his Son Jesus, and I for one am very grateful."

As they were talking, I was thinking about Olive and how glad I am that she is doing so well. Because of her fearful and understandable reaction to trucks, The Seeing Eye recommended that she live someplace away from all traffic. A number of people who knew her very much wanted her for a pet, and my master finally decided that the best place would be out in the country where she could live completely away from roads. That's where she is now, living on a farm with friends of our family who have two horses and another dog, and she is being extremely well taken care of.

I was so happy to have the chance to meet her last summer. I would never have known that she had been in an accident. She is absolutely beautiful, and her tail has grown in so thick you can't even tell she had surgery. She seems very happy there on the farm. As a matter of fact, I'm convinced that she thinks she finally found that fantastic party she was always looking for.

Because of his different obligations, it was five months until my master was able to get over to Morristown for another dog. When he arrived there, one of the administrators asked if he would be willing to serve on a panel with two of the other former graduates. They were to talk with a group of students from the University of Colorado who were learning to be mobility and orientation instructors. The three blind people sat with their dogs in front of those college students, and I guess I can slip in here that I was one of those proud dogs that day.

The other two speakers told their stories and experiences with their Seeing Eye dogs. When it came to be my new friend's turn, he shared with them some of his background and explained that I was his third dog. He made them laugh when he told them funny adventures that had happened with his canine buddies, and then he shifted to the story of Olive and the accident and how he felt responsible for it. Suddenly, for the first time and without any warning, he broke down. As tears ran down his face, the emotion of all that had happened truly hit him.

That night as he lay in bed, he tried to call Judy to let her know about his day's experiences; but then he remembered that she had told him that she'd be out. He was probably feeling as blue as he ever had over the accident, and I was glad to be there so that he felt a little less alone.

Not long after we got home from training, Olive's new family sent my master an email. Apparently she found a five-dollar bill that belonged to her mistress and promptly chewed it up and swallowed it. They wrote that it was proof to them that she had originally worked for a businessman and not to worry because they were going to wait a day and go outside to collect the change. I could see he loved reading that story, and it made him feel good to know that dear Olive was still up to her old tricks.

I have to tell you that, though I feel real compassion for Olive and for my friend because of the abrupt end to her career as a guide dog, it helps me to know how happy she is in her new home with loving people and all of those animal friends. It truly seems as if everything has turned out well for her, which eases my mind because, as you now know, I, Patton, was the dog that The Seeing Eye selected to take her place. Just about the time that she was in training with my master, my littermates and I had made our entrance into this beautiful world. Looking back, it seemed as if almost no time at all had passed before I was in the big house meeting that man with a cane that I wasn't too sure about at first. That initial reaction was soon replaced with other amazing feelings, for I think that my master and I bonded very quickly. I really do feel that we were meant to be a team; we're that perfect together.

I'd like to be able to say that from our first times out on our training runs at The Seeing Eye, I worked as hard as I could to please my new partner. But I've heard him say that I seemed a little sluggish in the beginning. His guess is that I was still waiting to have my trainer take me back to the life I had been leading before my friend and I became a team. Memories can be funny. Maybe I did feel that hesitation in the beginning, and maybe I wasn't quite ready to make the all-important transition to being a full-time guide dog with a man I was just getting to know. If that was true, it is hard for me to believe it now. Whatever exactly happened in those first days, I like to think I soon made up for it. Once I got into the groove, I wanted to lead him exactly as I'd been trained; and I never wanted to make a mistake. At the same time that my master mentioned I had been a little slow at the start, he also said that by the time we went home, I had it figured out.

I like this part that he said a lot, "Patton and I went home from The Seeing Eye with my trainer, and both of us were absolutely amazed by how well he did. It almost seemed as if he knew our route from home to work by instinct. He led me there without any hesitations; he even seemed to anticipate our turns. It felt as if he was so in tune with me that he sensed where I already knew we'd be heading. In fact his focus was so good that when a cat scurried across our path on that first walk, he ignored it completely. Then, unbelievably, a dog came running directly at us and slammed right into him. And, even with that, he didn't react at all. He just kept us moving forward. It was then I knew for sure that he is a truly extraordinary dog."

You can imagine how great those words make me feel, and they go a long way toward healing that little bit of hurt pride I felt when he referred to me as once being a little sluggish. But, of course, no matter how hard I've always tried to be perfect in my job, it's an impossible goal. Not too long ago I was thinking about our time in training, and I had the clearest memory of a day when I was trying to do my best at my job and it didn't turn out well.

How I remember it is that we were walking along and suddenly I heard a bang, followed by a loud, "Ouch!"

Oh darn, I thought, it must be another overhead; oh man, he corrects me on those. I realized he might be bleeding, but not too badly. I decided he'd be all right; I just wished I could find a way to see up high better than I do. I think I'm doing a good job, leading him, getting him where he needs to go; it's just that every once in awhile there are those low hanging branches or an awning at a store that are beyond my line of sight. Then I heard, "Hop up." We started going forward, so I guessed that meant that he was okay even though I caused him to get whacked.

Such mistakes didn't only happen when we were in training. Just the other day we went down to the corner and made a right turn, and we started down a pretty busy street where we came to a barrier. I stopped and the traffic was such that I couldn't go out and around the obstruction into the street. I wanted to go right across the grass on the other side of the barrier, but my buddy was reluctant to go that way. So I finally made the decision to go underneath. Unfortunately, that barrier caught him right at the waistline. We stopped very quickly; he corrected me and then we went back and sat down for a minute, and suddenly he realized that what I had wanted to do was the right thing and that he had tried to control the situation. Of course, I was trying to control it, too.

As we rested, I think both of us remembered that we are a unit; we are a team. So he petted me and gave me a hug, and I gave him a little nuzzle in return. Then we approached the barrier again; this time we went to the right and around on the grass down to the next barrier. Then we had to go left into the street, but there were cars coming. We patiently waited until it was clear, and we negotiated both of the obstructions. It's such a good thing that we can work with each other to get around the physical barriers in our path.

Now that I've gotten to know him so completely, I think in his own walk he has come to a number of barriers, not just physical ones but spiritual and emotional ones as well. Perhaps sometimes he has made some wrong choices, for after all, he is only human.

But what I've observed with him and other humans is that they sometimes don't seem able to let it go; they continue to remember a mistake. And because they remember, they continue to have self-pity; they keep thinking about what happened and use it as an excuse or let it weigh them down. It's unfortunate because God is there, and God says that if you repent He forgives. I've learned that, and I'm just a dog.

You see, there are dogs in training that just don't make it through the whole process to become Seeing Eye graduates. I think that, except for those that might have health issues and just can't perform because of those problems, the dogs that don't make it can't learn how to accept forgiveness after correction. The correction itself devastates them and then, even the "Atta boy" or "Atta girl" doesn't resonate with them; and they can't bounce back. It seems that can happen even with graduate dogs if what they see as a correction is severe. I think that's what the trainers at The Seeing Eye meant about Olive because they've seen it with other dogs, too. For them the restoration is blocked, and so it is sometimes with human beings.

I know my buddy can get angry with me sometimes, but I also know he never holds on to it for long. There are times, too, when we both can get a little confused, and that can lead to funny circumstances. One night we had been out to a meeting, and another member offered us a ride home. As he drove away, we went to the front yard for my last park time of the evening. After being there a minute, we heard our neighbor, who is also a good friend, call to us. The two men chatted for a minute, and then our friend went on his way. Once I was finished my business, we headed up to the front door. It was when we reached the stoop that my master realized that we weren't at our house after all. I had known we were in our friend's yard, which is down the street from ours; but I thought we had just stopped there for a minute. The man who gave us the ride had never been to our house before, and I guess he misunderstood where we lived. After my friend had a good chuckle, he directed me to go home; and soon we were settled in for the night.

Chapter Fifteen

Amazing grace how sweet the sound that saved a wretch like me. I once was lost but now am found, was blind but now I see. John Newton

Actually, once my friend and I went home from The Seeing Eye, every day became an adventure for me. I learned the routes that he needed to travel most of the time, and I learned to match my pace to his so that we'd both be comfortable walking. I have to say that I love my job. One time I heard someone saying to my master that he felt a little sorry for me because I had to work and couldn't be a family pet like most dogs are. I wished I could speak, so I could have explained to him that I like my life very much exactly as it is. The other thing is that there already is a pet in our house, and it seems to me that for us one is enough.

After I had been with them a few months, my friend and Judy decided that I would be fine living with another dog. Sometimes it doesn't work out too well if there are pets living in the same place as a guide dog, but they thought I'd be all right with it. Judy, who you know has always been the real dog lover, was missing having a pet of her own now that she no longer had Trevor. She decided on getting a Boxer like she had as a child, and that's when Banner entered our life. She was such a cute little thing when she first came home. She also needed to learn manners, as is the case with all puppies. I've always tried to be gentle with her, but I also wanted to set a good example of how she should learn to behave. I've never let her roughhouse inside our house; I made that clear from the beginning.

But we do have fun out in our fenced-in yard. We play games where she runs around and around in circles, and I go with her. Sometimes I play a trick on her and cut her off in her track, but its all good-natured fun that we both like a lot. We eat our meals together, and we've never had any problems with that. Trying to be a gentleman, I always wait for her to finish her chow before I eat mine. When it's my turn, she never tries to eat from my bowl; but once I'm finished she'll give it a few little licks. Banner goes everywhere with my master's wife, and sometimes we ride in the car at the same time.

Even though she does go everywhere with her mistress, Banner doesn't lead her. She is a pet and a companion, and what we're expected to do is different. That's fine with us; she likes her life just as I like mine, and both of us enjoy having some canine company. Occasionally, but fortunately not too often, we both have to sleep in our crates; and I like it that hers is right next to mine. When I'm not on duty, we're good company for each other.

As I've said, what I like best is working for my good buddy; yes, guiding his way is my favorite thing to do. And you wouldn't believe how much time off I have to rest and relax. Take right now as an example. I woke up a few minutes ago and found the house all quiet around me even though there's a little early light outside. I guess my master's getting some extra rest this morning. If I wanted to, I could drift on back to sleep myself. Or I can just lie here and daydream a bit; except, to tell the truth, pretty soon I'm going to need to get outside for a short park time. Oh good, now I hear him and thank goodness, he's waking up. Okay, I'm hoping he's getting dressed because all of a sudden I don't know how much longer I can hold it.

Ahhh, good, we're going downstairs and we're going out back. Great, here we go. Whew! I'm sure glad that he loves me, and I'm very glad about how well he understands all of my needs. I wonder if he knows how much I love him? I mean, I would really do anything for him because every morning we get up, we go outside, and then we go back in the house just like today. Now he's fixing me a good breakfast, and he's giving me some fresh, cool water. Once I've eaten, he'll brush and comb me so I look and feel my best. This is how we get ready for our day. Pretty soon he'll spend a little time doing his own exercises; and I'm happy to lie here and watch because when he's done, I know that we'll be going for a walk. He really does know exactly what I need all of the time.

Oh good, his exercises on those funny clanking machines didn't take too long; and now he's getting the leash and harness ready, putting the harness on me, and here we go. All right! I wonder where we're going today? We're headed out the front door, and turning left, down to the corner to the traffic light. We have to wait for the traffic, and I have to wait for him to tell me when to move.

Okay, just wait, until, "Patton, forward."

For a minute, I thought we might be going to church because it's right on this corner, close to our house, and we go there a lot; but it looks as if today we're going to keep moving instead of going in the door.

The short journey to church always takes place on Sunday mornings. My master and Judy and I walk there together, and then we go down the steps to the basement where we participate in something called Sunday school. In this meeting, a group of people gathers together and studies particular passages of Scripture. I like to be there; I get to lie down and listen while they talk.

We usually have to leave a little bit before the discussion is completed because we go over to the choir room for my master to put on his robe and practice a song for the church service with the other members of the choir. Then we go upstairs to the choir loft, where he usually takes my harness off so there's more room for me under the benches where he and the other choir members sit. I like how they harmonize beautiful anthems of praise to God. One of my favorite hymns goes like this, "Turn your eyes upon Jesus, look full in His wonderful face, and the things of earth will grow strangely dim in the light of his glory and grace."

Yes, grace, what a wonderful word that is, the ability to know that we are forgiven and that our mistakes will not be held against us. Ah, if I could just be perfect; but I know it's not going to happen. I think my friend has the same feeling that I have and struggles sometimes to forgive himself. I know that feeling. Sometimes when I make a mistake and get the correction, it's like Ahhh, I just feel so bad. And I need that, "Atta boy, Patton," so much. Fortunately, my master is quick to give that to me when I get back on the right path and the right focus.

But I watch people, and I think it's harder for them to forgive themselves. You know it's not like God is standing right beside them in a physical sense, and saying, "Atta boy, all is well." No, it's more subtle for people; and they have to search for an understanding of how God speaks to him. For some, it may be through music; for others, it might be through reading The Scriptures. I think one of the things that's important for these humans is that they need to learn to express and share God's Grace in order to reinforce each other in forgiving themselves. It would be wonderful if everyone around them would immediately say, "Atta boy, or Atta girl, you're okay; we all have our pitfalls. Don't give up, keep running, keep trying, keep searching, keep singing, and keep praying. It's okay." If I could talk to people, that's what I'd tell them. It's wonderful to see when people come to a point of trusting the grace given by God and then pass it on to someone else.

There are several occasions in the service when the choir members stand up and then sit down. They pray and read Scripture, and then the man they all call the pastor gets up and talks about Jesus and how each of us has the need for Him to be our Savior. He talks about how to apply parts of The Scripture readings in our lives today. I say *our* because now that I'm connected to my master, I try to follow his spiritual vocation and growth pretty much most of the time, especially because it's so much a part of my friend's life. Sometimes, after church, we go up to one of the restaurants in town and have a bite to eat after the service, which I like to do.

We also go to the church at other times during the course of the week. On Wednesday nights, there is choir practice; and sometimes there are social functions at church that are a lot of fun. Usually there is food involved, and that gets a little tempting sometimes, especially with the kids walking around with those little morsels that are just at my level. But you've got to watch that temptation stuff, especially when you're at church.

Sometimes, too, my buddy might go to the church for a meeting; those are usually held in what they call the library, which is a small room where they have couches and chairs; and there are books and tapes for the people to check out and read in their spare time. Every once in awhile there will be a breakfast meeting down at the church, and we'll go to those. Recently, my master has been involved in something they call the men's ministry where there is a breakfast and a speaker afterwards. Yes, I guess you could say we spend a lot of good times at our church.

But now that I know we're not going to church this morning, I'm curious where we're headed; we've crossed Fifth Street, then straight down Market, and it looks as if we're going toward the walking path. On our way, I notice what a wonderful morning this is. Now that we're almost there, I feel a beautiful, cool breeze coming through the trees with the sound of the stream flowing right along in its cheerful way. We have to cross the stream first across a little walking bridge, and we make the right turn on to the path. Now I can hear the water gurgling to our right, and that sound makes me feel happy.

Hooray! I just realized we're taking one of our longer routes today, and that means it isn't a workday. That makes me even happier. It's not that I mind going to work. Everyone there is always kind to me, and I get to rest a lot during all the meetings. But I still like the days we don't go to work even better.

Ouch! I hate when he has to correct me; I guess I've been letting my mind wonder. I've got to pay a little more attention to my job.

"Atta boy, atta boy; good job, Patton." Oh, those are good words to hear; now I just have to stay focused. There's a squirrel, but I'm not looking! I'm not going to pay any attention to it at all.

Well, here we are returning from our walk, and we've had a great time. I'm kind of pausing a little to see what's next. Some mornings we stop along the way at our café where my master will have a cup of coffee and a doughnut or maybe even a big breakfast; and then we'll head on home. Other days we go straight home, for by now the sun is up and Judy is awake. I know she'll be so glad to see me and that she'll be waiting to greet me with hugs and pets. I wonder which way we'll go this morning.

It might seem to some people that my friend always lives in a world that's utterly dark, that everything is black for him. It may be that his blindness could be thought of that way; but I honestly believe his life is filled with a great deal of light. I like to think that I add a lot of brightness to his life, partly through helping him maneuver through his world with confidence. I also hope, and do sincerely believe, that my devotion to him and our great friendship brighten his world; but I'm only one part of the picture. Actually, one of the many things I really like about him is that he's always open to ways to illuminate his life.

I suppose, once he started losing his vision, he could have just kind of given up and thought, "Okay. I'm blind and everything is dark; and I wish it hadn't happened, but that's just how my life is now."

Instead, from the very beginning of his losing his sight, he has looked for ways to maintain light in his life; and because he has always stood up to the darkness and the fears it can bring, he has continued to do almost all of the things he would have done if he had remained fully sighted. Learning to work with guide dogs is, to me, just one way he has stood up to the darkness that could have overwhelmed him if he had allowed it to.

Some of the light that I see shining for him in the physical sense has to do with the technologies that exist today to assist blind people in being able to read and communicate by way of computers with the use of a devise known as a screen reader. This tool enables them to be able to have access to texts of almost any sort, the use of websites, and just about any other function that can be accomplished on a computer. Special programming can then read the information aloud through a synthesizer and voice card. These screen readers also enable the blind individual to send and receive email and to be able to perform both word processing and spreadsheets.

It's fascinating for me to watch my master communicate with some of his friends through the computer almost as easily as a sighted person. Actually, I don't completely understand all of how this technical stuff works or the varying forms it takes, and I know that even he is still learning them; but as his vision diminished, he focused on making the most of those technologies that he needed as they were developed. It's lucky for him that they came about just at the time he needed them. The advances they are making include ever-smaller devices which allow blind men and women to carry scanners to meetings for reading handouts and other documents; this particular development makes it possible for blind individuals to be a part of the sighted world in a lot of different ways. My buddy's continued success in the business world was partially made possible because of these great inventions. But as great as they are, even these advances make up just one piece of the light that my master brings into his world.

The development over the years of Braille as a method for blind individuals to be able to read has been of great assistance to the visually impaired community for a long time, long before computers were invented. It's a system in which reading is done, not by your eyes, but by running the tips of your fingers over groups of dots that are embossed on a page. This clever tool was invented almost two hundred years ago by a Frenchman named Louis Braille who became blind himself when he was a boy.

Being able to read in this way requires the blind individual to develop a touch for as well as a memory of the system; actually, Braille text can be utilized by anyone who trains himself to understand it. My friend can read it, and he is continuing to study the more advanced Braille texts that are available to him. Although you might think that modern technology would have replaced this older method, blind people still need to know at least enough Braille to be able to label files and negotiate in hotels and elevators. Lots of public places provide information through those little dots that are arranged to mean words, and probably most sighted people don't even notice that they're there.

Modern inventors are continuing to build on this technique, and a Braille format can now be put into a computer which then reads it aloud. There are devices that allow blind people to take notes in this way as well as through voice audio output, and there are enhancements available for computers that can actually put information into Braille format. Something tells me that the man who came up with this technique was pretty good at looking for the light in his blindness, too; and I'd bet he'd be impressed with how far his invention has come since his day.

As I watch my friend negotiating through the darkness while searching for the light that is available to him, it seems it is definitely a great help to be able to have both technology and Braille. But as important as they are to him, what I see as another, and possibly more important way that he seeks light, is in his many friendships. The trust and the bond that I have with my master help to overcome the darkness that he has in this world in the physical sense, and the friendship of his true friends, as expressed in the many daily encounters with them, helps him to overcome the loneliness of that darkness. But he, too, has a role in this; he has a role as he reaches back.

For the most part, it is my observation that all humans have the capacity to reach outside of their darkness and to accept the light that comes to them through their relationships. In addition to all of his long-term friendships, some of which go all the way back to his childhood, he continues to be open to the light of making new friends as well. Often these new people in his life provide him with opportunities to learn and opportunities to gain an appreciation for the lives of others. I think this one example might help me explain what I mean. My master recently met a couple who have the same eye disease as he does; and along with this disease, they also have something called Usher's Syndrome, which unfortunately occurs for some R.P. victims. With this condition, they have a loss of hearing as well as visual loss over time.

I've seen my friend's compassion for this couple that, like the famous Helen Keller, not only are unable to see but also are unable to hear. I can only imagine how devastating it must be to become both blind and deaf while having a talented mind that functions just as well as ever in spite of the limitations of impaired communications. Both my master and I are impressed with the things that these people are able to do and what they can accomplish. Imagine not being able to see or hear, to be totally locked out. Knowing how my buddy can feel so alone sometimes when he can't appreciate what others are looking at around him, I can't imagine what it must be like for these people. And yet, I've also heard wonderful things about Helen Keller who couldn't see or hear from childhood but who became world-famous as a writer and as a champion for other people with disabilities. If you ask me, she is a wonderful example of incorporating beauty and purpose into a world that could have been both dark and silent; and my master's friends have that same admirable quality.

Chapter Sixteen

*No one lights a lamp and hides it in a jar or puts it under
a bed. Instead, he puts it on a stand, so that those who
come in can see the light.   Luke 8:16*

It seems to me that all of my master's friendships have a lot of
value in many different ways; and the things that he has been able to
do and accomplish because of those relationships, I think, might be
more important to shedding light into his life than all the technology
and Braille in the world. But I don't mean to make it all sound too
serious, especially because I've noticed in the friendship between
human beings that often they express their feelings by kidding with
and needling each other. That kind of fun can sure cause a whole lot
of laughter. The light-hearted needling part, from what I've seen, is
not as true for women in their relationships with other women as it is
very much a part of men's relationships with other men. But I have to
be careful here about what I say about any differences between men
and women; I'm sure not going to open that can of worms. Yet I do
think that, especially for men, all that kidding around is part of how
they express their liking and love for each other. Actually, I've heard
my buddy say, and I believe it's true, that even our relationship with
God is intended to have some of those same qualities.

He explains it like this, "Our friendship with our Lord should be
so strong and so real that we recognize that he, too, has a sense of
humor and that it's okay to be able to laugh at some of our own
mistakes and to laugh at some of the things in nature that are quite
honestly humorous. I think that God intended for a lot of things to
bring a smile to our faces."

And so it seems to follow that, if my friend is created in the
image of God, it should not be surprising that there are fun and
laughter, and the ability to have enough confidence in our friendships
with each other to be able to kid and tease in good humor.

I heard my master talking about this question one day with some of his friends, or maybe it was at Sunday school; anyway, this is what he had to say, "So, does God have a sense of humor? I believe so; after all, he put Jonah in the belly of a whale for three days before Jonah went on to do the Lord's will. He sent David as a freckle-faced boy out to defeat Goliath. He empowered Samson to defeat and slay thousands of Philistines with the jaw of a donkey. He watched from onshore as Peter and John and the others unsuccessfully fished all day and all night and then allowed their net to become so full they could barely get it onto the boat. He used Rahab, the prostitute, to hide the spies in Jericho and then allowed her to marry into the Jewish nation and become part of the line to our Savior and Lord Jesus Christ. Over and over again God's sense of humor and His desire for us to see His power in the least of all things is revealed."

It makes me think that perhaps even in my buddy's life, his sense of humor is often an empowerment for seeing the light. I've heard him make little jokes that I think help to put both him and others at ease concerning his vision. Should we be surprised if God wants us to have fun? Should we be surprised that God brings the haughty and proud down and allows the least to be first, as I've heard at church? I think not; after all, look how he uses a mere dog like me to guide a creation that He said He made just a little bit in His own image.

Telling this story about my friend and his thoughts on God's sense of humor is a reminder to me of the all-powerful source of light that his faith has provided throughout his life, both in the time he had sight and through all of the potentially dark days since then. How many times have I heard him say that his faith has gotten him through his darkest moments? And of all the ways that God has both blessed and brightened his life, the most important of all is through the great love that he shares with his wife and with the family that they created together. The closeness that they all share is absolutely central to his life and happiness. And I think through watching them I've also come to understand his relationship with God a little better because it seems to me that the closest we can come to understanding God's love for his children is through knowing the love that parents feel for their own children.

My master's own words tell it best: "Of all the things that I've done in life, being a father and now a grandfather are the most important, the most challenging, and most exciting of all things that I've known. Although the other things are important, how can I tell you how it feels to be loved and to love our oldest daughter who will always be our first child, and our second daughter who has blessed us with grandchildren, and our son who carries my name? I am proud of each one of them, for they all are talented and compassionate: Kelly as a nurse caring for people and now helping them through her research; Kris whose life is dedicated to her family and her church community shows her caring heart for those around her; and David who works so well with children who have trouble in the regular cultural setting of public schools. They are all enormously talented; and even more importantly, they are truly good people."

Looking back from the time they were very small, my good friend has talked about his role as a father, "It's hard to believe that these three fine adults were once little children who were put in our charge, Judy's and mine, to teach, to help, and to take care of; so that someday they would be able to go forward and take their talents and the things they have learned and share the gifts that they have. Now they help others beyond themselves to also grow; they deeply care about them, while still caring for each other and our family.

"As I look back, I sometimes ask myself: how did I do as a parent? Like most parents, I think I was often a good father and sometimes not a good father. My deep voice could always get their attention, and sometimes I used my physical presence to get my children to obey me. But did I always handle every situation in the best way? Of course not. There were times that I was overbearing and insisted on my way without always giving a fair hearing to my children's concerns or laments. I suppose in ways I regret some of that. Actually, I'm sure I do; but the truth is that love and trust overcome our mistakes. If we're true to that love and trust, they will allow the child and the parent to soon forget any offense."

As my master readily admits, being human, the family hasn't always been absolutely perfect. From what I see, they are all perfect enough; but I guess they've had their moments of upset as well. They joke about it now, but the children did have their share of spats when they were growing up. And as it is in almost all families, there's always been a little healthy sibling rivalry, you know, the familiar, "Oh mom and dad loved you more. Look what they gave you. Look what they did for you." Though I'm not a parent, it seems to me that when you're raising children it's difficult some times; you want to treat them all fairly and within certain boundaries. But they are all distinct and unique individuals; and because of that, their needs and their wants will vary. My guess is that the best you can do is treat them each in accord with their personalities and their needs.

I've heard my friend compare this question of fair treatment of his three children with God's relationship to His children, and he asks, "Does God treat each of us the same? Of course not, we are each created with our own talents, abilities, and personalities that allow for us to focus on specific roles. I think of how it is said in The Scriptures about the church and the body of believers and how each of us has different talents that we take to the party. I mean, can the foot say to the hand: I don't need you; or can the hand say to the leg: we don't need you? No, of course not. Just as The Scriptures say, this is all blended together, each with a specific purpose. I think it's much the same with our own children. Just as each of them is special, each of them is also unique."

From my first days here at home, I've known his whole family well. They are all always great to me, and I've grown to love them almost as I do him. I really like being part of their gatherings and getting to hear the family stories. I don't know if it's true for all families; but for this one, they have a strong bond created by trust and love that makes them rally together when any one of them needs help or support. It's almost like a circling of the wagons back in the old westerns. That's a very nice thing, and it makes me a happy pup to be a part of it.

From the stories I've heard, Kelly, that first precious baby, was always sensitive and in tune with what was happening around her. Part of Kelly's personality has been for her to be quite introspective and insightful, and she's approached things in a rather analytical way. At a recent family dinner, her dad, my master, was reminiscing about her as a child; it's a story that, I think, shows something of what Kelly has always been like, even as a little girl.

"As you all know," my friend began, "Parents need to be aware that our children are always around, and we always tried to be careful about what we were saying or talking about in your presence. And one day you, Kelly, were lying on the couch in the living room, and your mom and I were in the midst of a conversation. And it came to one of those points when you suddenly stop the conversation to make sure who might be around, and one of us said, 'Where's Kelly?' And the other one said, 'I think she's in here on the couch.' 'Oh yes, there she is, she's there sleeping.' Then Kelly said, 'I'm not asleep.' And your mother asked, 'Then what are you doing?' Kelly responded, "I'm just here peeking my eyes out.' Kelly was," my master added, "Always aware, I think, of our conversations and therefore had a questioning mind about what was happening around her."

Then the conversation moved to Kris, and everyone agreed that she was the most active one; she was always climbing trees and on the monkey bars at the playground. Her mom had great difficulty even trying to put Kris into a dress to go to school or church because of how active she was. At any moment you'd find her standing on her hands, doing cartwheels, or going hand over hand on the monkey bars. Those early skills paid off for her when she was older and earned a full scholarship to college as a gymnast.

One of my favorite stories about Kris took place when she was in fifth grade, and she became a part of the safety control program. Her particular corner, where it was her responsibility to help the younger children cross safely, was at the entrance to the elementary school and its parking lot. Every morning she would go out to her assigned station, and it was not unusual for people to tell her parents that they saw her standing on her hands or doing a cartwheel into the corner in between the times she needed to direct the younger children across to school. That was Kris, always active and on the move even while standing on her hands. One morning she went down to her post and soon afterwards the family's phone rang and her dad answered it.

One of the neighbors across the street, who happened to be able to see Kris' corner, was on the line; and she said, "John, I'm calling because I'm concerned that Kris may not be feeling well today."

"Really?" he asked, "What makes you say that?"

She answered, "Well, I've been watching her all morning and she hasn't stood on her hands or done a single cartwheel. She's just standing there quietly and doing her job."

Sure enough by lunchtime that day, Kris was sent home from school because she was sick.

From their stories, it seems to me that people tend to remember things from when they were children as being bigger than life; the snows of their childhoods are deeper, the rains are harder, the hot summer days are even hotter than anything they now experience. I think probably what they remember is those special days, that major snowstorm or that one big rain and wind event that was the tail end of an unusual hurricane moving through the area.

Thinking about this, my friend told another story that same night, "For you two girls I'm pretty sure that one of the things you remember is that huge snowstorm we had on a Friday; your school was closed and even the employees where I worked were sent home early. As I remember, I arrived home, and the storm kept on raging. You girls wanted to have take-out hoagies for dinner. I told you that I couldn't drive because the streets were almost closed over, but you two said that you would walk into town."

Kelly added, "Of course I remember that day. We got bundled up and left the house to walk that half-mile into town, and we did get those hoagies. Then we walked back toward home in what had to be one of the biggest blizzards in my memory. It was so great; we were walking down the middle of the street since there was no traffic, and the snow was piling up and the wind was driving against us."

Then Kris added, "That snow was plastering into our faces. And all of that just to get our sandwiches for the night!" Then she added, "It's funny that story came up again now." And she turned to her sister and her mom, "Do you remember when we were just talking about this?"

They then recounted the story of when the two of them and their mother and Kris' daughter had recently gone to New York City for a trip, they ate at a restaurant where there was a little centerpiece from which you pulled a question.

The question they got was, "What is your fondest winter memory?" And both girls had immediately answered, "The time we walked to town to get hoagies in the blizzard." There are, I'm sure, many other memories of winter that they must have because they did lots of sledding and other cold weather activities, but for them that walk in the snowstorm had been the great adventure of their young lives.

"Speaking of favorite family stories, " Judy added, "I used to love the way David would play with Kindle and how much she loved to play with him. Remember how he would play football and all kinds of games in the backyard with her, and she thought that was the greatest thing that ever happened?"

She turned to David, "And I think maybe you did, too. You would run into the house and say, 'Kindle's ahead by one touchdown. But it's halftime so there's still hope.' Then you'd get a drink of water or milk and cookies, and after your snack you'd go back out to continue the game with your favorite opponent, Kindle the Golden Retriever."

"I hadn't thought of that for awhile," David answered with a smile. "She really was a great dog. I think in all of our games we were pretty well tied. But maybe I'm giving myself a little too much credit. Maybe she ended up ahead most of the time."

I have to admit that I like the idea of another dog, a creature like me, being remembered as a winner in games with the wonderful little boy that David must have been, no matter which of them actually did have more points.

That story about David reminds me of how important sports have always been in this family. And it makes me think about a pretty important activity that my buddy has recently taken on. A while ago, when I was talking about the adjustments he had needed to make, one of the things that I mentioned was how he had to give up playing baseball, which as you know had been his first love in sports.

It just wasn't possible for him to continue playing that All-American game though he has continued to follow it avidly both through his family members who also are really into it and by listening to professional games on television and the radio. But being a devoted fan is never quite the same as being in there in the grass and the dirt, participating yourself. Not being directly involved in sports at some level would have been too much of a loss for someone who found so much fun and satisfaction through them, so he focused on other athletic outlets.

For some time he was able to continue to play both tennis and golf. Unfortunately, as his vision narrowed he had to give up tennis because of the speed and pace and movement of the ball. Then for a while more he was able to play golf. He could still be playing that game; as a matter of fact, to this day there is a blind golf association. But because of the friendships that had been extended and ultimately shared, he has focused for the last few years on a couple of different sports. And if you know much about them at all, the fact that he's an enthusiastic participant may surprise you a little.

When my friend and I were in training, he came in contact with two other blind people who talked to him about a group called Ski for Light, more commonly known as SFL. This organization was created more than forty years ago to encourage blind and mobility-impaired individuals to learn how to cross country ski. When he was first approached about getting involved with the organization, my master thought it might be a great idea, until he remembered the fact that he had never skied in any way in his life, not downhill nor cross country. He had never even had the sensation of standing on skis much less moving down a trail on them. Now that he was blind some well-meaning people thought he could go out and learn how to ski.

The idea was so crazy that he decided to give it a try. After all, I've heard him say, what did he have to lose? As I've mentioned he always keeps himself open to new possibilities for staying in the world and allowing in the light, but talk about trust. If he'd asked me, I probably would have told him it was a crazy idea for a blind man, especially one who isn't exactly a boy any more, to take on a sport that's potentially a little dangerous even for fully sighted young people. Now he probably wouldn't like that I said that part about his not being a boy; and the truth is that he's in great shape, actually better than lots of people who are younger than he is. So let's just forget I made that comment.

And so it came to be that on a cold February day, my friend, Judy, and I, flew to Colorado, got on a bus and traveled over Bertha's Pass at 11,000 feet above sea level, across the Continental Divide, and then to a small town named Granby, Colorado. It was there, along with more than a hundred other blind and ten mobility-impaired skiers, as well as a the same number of sighted guides, that my master was about to embark on a trust experience that would entail learning how to cross country ski.

The ski resort areas where the SFL people go establish cross-country trails, and they lay down tracks so that the skiers work their skis in grooves laid through many kilometers of trails. There are actually two sets of tracks, one for the blind or mobility-impaired skier and the other for the sighted guide. Generally, the sighted guide will be in the tracks immediately to the left of his partner skier; and this guide will be giving instructions as to what is ahead that they should anticipate, whether the track goes to the left or the right, or whether there is a downhill or uphill grade. They also tell their partner when to anticipate having to herringbone, which is a technique to climb hills that are steeper; and they tell them when it will be necessary to control their speed by snow plowing when a downhill is steep.

In the course of skiing on these trails, it's sometimes necessary to pass slower skiers; in that case, the sighted guide will then either move ahead or behind his skier and instruct him to track left and then place his skis in the left side track in order to pass. Different sighted guides use their own methods of being beside, behind, or ahead of their skiers; it all depends on the skill level of the skier and also sometimes of the ability of the sighted guide. But basically, each day for one week, the skier with the sighted guide gets the opportunity to ski through the trails.

In some cases, people will do as little as two kilometers in a run; others will go to five or ten or even more kilometers. At the end of the week, there are two races on what is known among the participants as Race Rally Day. In the five kilometer run, each skier picks his time; and the winner is the one who comes closest to the goal without going over his predicted time for five kilometers. The other is a straight out race in which the skiers are seeded by their ability; this is a ten kilometer race with winners being awarded in categories that are determined by partial sight, total blindness, and age categories. The mobility-impaired skiers, who use what is known as sit skis, have different criteria. In a ten kilometer race, the very slowest skiers take two and a half to three hours to complete the racecourse; occasionally people take even more time. The fastest of the skiers will complete the course in just under an hour, somewhere between forty-five and fifty-five minutes. That can be a very fast time depending on the course itself and the difficulty of the hills.

That first year my master, having never skied in any fashion before, had quite a lot to learn; and he tells a lot of funny stories about some of the positions that he assumed while learning to snowplow on the downhill parts of the course. He also talks about the face plants that he experienced during that week; but as he tells it, as the week progressed he gained more and more confidence. By the end of the week on that first trip, he competed in the five kilometer rally and predicted a time of one hour and fifteen minutes. On that Race Rally Day, he actually completed the course in an hour and three minutes. This run didn't put him in any prize category, but he was pleased with the fact that he got close to skiing five kilometers in one hour. More importantly, he had found his new sport.

Chapter Seventeen

He leadeth Me, O Blessed Thought   Joseph H. Gilmore

I've often heard my friend talk about those first days of learning how to ski. He excitedly describes the joy and freedom that he found after he finally got his legs under him, but let's let him tell you about it.

"There I was in the middle of The Colorado Rocky Mountains meeting my guide, Rob, who was of Norwegian descent and had lived his whole life it seemed on skis. As a matter of fact, he owned a ski and bicycle shop. We went out to the lodge where the trails began, and he picked out the skis and boots that I had rented for the week. As I was putting my boots on, he said to me, 'Have you ever been on skis before?'

"'No,' I answered. 'I have never, ever been on skis.'

"'Oh good, this should really be exciting,' was his response.

"And so, after I had the boots on we went outside. And I have to say, it was scary. I was thinking, is this ever going to be embarrassing. I put my boots into the bindings, and then, miraculously, I was standing on two skis.

"'Just slide them forward,' he told me. 'Slide one in front of the other.'

"With that we began to walk forward. And now I was thinking, 'Holy cow, maybe I can do this.'

"But after we had gone about a hundred feet, I just kind of lost my balance and slowly fell over to one side. My new thought was, 'I can't even stand up on these things.'

"Rob looked at me and said, 'Hmmm, okay. Get yourself back up.'

"We got out to the spot where the trails began, and he told me we were going to work on some fundamentals.

"'The first thing I want you to do is fall down,' Rob told me, and he didn't sound like he was joking.

"'Excuse me?'

"'That's right, I want you to fall down,' he repeated

"I thought, 'Now, that won't be hard. I did it a minute ago with no effort at all.' And so I fell down on the snow, and he proceeded to teach me how to get back up with those long planks on my feet. I realized then how important it was to know how to get back up, how to get those skis back under you. Then we worked on the positioning of the body and the bending of the knees in relation to where you are over your skis.

"Just as I would think I was getting the position right, he'd say, 'No, not like that, try this.'

"'I'm sorry,' was my response. Actually I said I'm sorry every time I didn't do exactly as he said, until finally he gave me a little friendly whack with his ski pole.

"'You've got to stop saying 'I'm sorry.' You're learning from the beginning here; you don't have anything to be sorry about. We're here to teach you.'

"We continued to work, standing still, and I made myself stop saying that I was sorry. From there, we went to the place where there were practice tracks laid out in the snow, about a hundred and fifty meters in length with straight, level runs. Rob skied along beside me as I first learned the scissors kick and then double poling. After about three or four times on that flat surface, I started to feel some semblance of confidence. I was standing up and sliding and actually moving forward in the tracks.

"Unfortunately, my guide was experiencing a flu bug, and we could only stay out for the morning that first day. By the end of the week, at least half of the participants had that virus.

"On the second day, although I was still feeling a little apprehensive, I was excited to get out there and try again. Though Rob was not feeling well, he was determined for us to put in another lesson; so we worked together in the morning. We went out for a short run and we came to a little bend to the right with a slight downhill. It was my first downhill, and I went to the bottom of the dip and started back up.

"Suddenly it was as if the tips of my skis had hit a stone wall. The skis stopped dead, but my body kept going; and I experienced my very first face plant. I was to find out that face plants are part of cross country skiing; however, when you experience the first one, it really is quite a jolt, especially when you can't see the ground coming up at you. My nose felt as if it was broken; but I stood back up, and my guide being the indomitable instructor that he is, looked at me and said, 'Good. Now we got that out of the way.'

"Needless to say, I was going slowly and still just learning, but I was experiencing the beginning of that amazing feeling of freedom. After lunch, Rob was still unwell, so I worked with a wonderful young woman named Winnie who came from Georgia. We did probably three kilometers, and I was starting to know the exhilaration of movement that comes when you are on skis. On the third day Winnie stayed with me, and she taught me to herringbone on the up trails. The down hills, which require snowplowing, were still giving me a little trouble. We had a kind of funny moment when Winnie took me to a practice hill. The first time I skied down without her right beside me, and I suddenly found myself on my right ski with my left one way up in the air. I tried to pull the ski down without getting the heel in the snow; but that didn't work and I wound up going over backwards, slamming my head with my knit cap flying. Winnie came swishing down to check to see if I was still in one piece.

"'That must have looked pretty,' I told her as I struggled back up.

"'I just wish I had a camera,' she laughed with relief.

"Every day I gained confidence and experienced more and more freedom and exhilaration. I mean, blind people don't go for a run across a field. But now I, on skis, had the thrill of running in track with a guide right beside me. That feeling of athleticism was right there for me again."

That first year on skis he learned a lot about listening and trusting, and a quite a bit of it sounds very familiar to me. For when he walks with me and I guide him, he has to listen for the traffic around him and for particular sounds that will help him determine where he is. At the same time, he has to pay attention to the slope of the sidewalk or the number of blocks that we've gone, so that he has an idea of his orientation and can know when it's time to turn left or right at the next corner. Most importantly, he must trust me because I have to be looking for where he wants to go, and I have to pick up on where there is an object that's a barrier or something that's in our way. In such cases, he follows me as I guide him around it.

From what I've heard these skiers say, it's similar with cross-country skiing as he listens to the sighted guide, this time a person. He has to pay attention to staying in the track, leaning to the left or right as the track turns, or using the herringbone or snowplow when they're required. All of this happens while he's adjusting his speed and control and following the instructions of the sighted guide through these different maneuvers. In some cases, the guide goes ahead where there is no track; and my master must listen for the voice of the guide as he follows and turns and moves toward that voice to get back into the track.

The second year that my master went to Ski for Light it was also held in Granby, Colorado; and he was fortunate to get a very experienced guide named Jeannie who lived in that state. She was both an excellent skier and guide. They set as their goal for the week to be able to compete in the ten kilometer race, and so my friend set out to accomplish the task of completing a course that was twice as long as he had skied the year before. The good news is that at the end of that week they were able to meet their goal in one hour and forty-four minutes. Although that may not be considered a particularly fast time, it was good enough to show improvement in my master's skiing and in giving him the sense of accomplishment which came from listening to his guide and trusting in her instruction.

The following year Ski for Light was held in New Hampshire, but unfortunately the course they had intended to use just hadn't had enough snow during that mild winter. They were forced to use trails that didn't allow for a Race Rally Day. But then the next year, the event was held in Bend, Oregon where there was plenty of snow as well as plenty of trails. They were difficult trails; in fact, they were some of the most challenging courses for even the most experienced of skiers. This time my buddy was paired with a young man who was guiding for the first time. Although he was a good skier, he was still learning the techniques of how to guide someone who was visually impaired. This inexperience lead to some interesting circumstances along the way; and unfortunately, it created some doubt in my master's mind.

Now I'm sure you can understand that when you're in a situation where you have to trust your Seeing Eye dog or your sighted guide in skiing or your friend while negotiating in a new place, if something happens to create doubt in your mind, it changes everything.

My master describes this loss of trust in this way, "You lose confidence and suddenly you're not skiing quite as fast, you're not walking as fast, and you may even become reluctant to go out at all. This is not too dissimilar in our spiritual lives. If something happens, perhaps even our own sin, that may cause us to doubt the existence or the viability of our Lord and Savior, suddenly we are reluctant to trust. When that happens, we are hampered in our living in just about everything we do. Maybe we even get to the point that we become afraid to go out, and suddenly we don't know what to do. We lose our orientation, and how can we regain what is lost? When you're skiing, how do you regain the confidence and the trust? "

That year's skiing experience had some ups and downs in regard to that all-important trust factor; and unfortunately, it ended with my master's getting out of track and experiencing a near calamity. From what I've heard him tell his friends, the combination of wanting to go faster, a difficult course, and a new guide probably set up the scene for trouble.

"There we were at the last major downhill of a ten kilometer race, with about two and a half kilometers to go to the finish," my friend explained. "I had been jerky at the start, and I had just started to smooth things out and get some rhythm. I probably should have stayed in track, but I made the decision with my guide to move out and snowplow down the terrain. In track you have a little more control, and you have the benefit of knowing exactly where you are. In the snowplow position you can control your speed, but that's when the communication between you and your sighted guide becomes critical.

"Hindsight is, as they say, perfect; and now I realize I should have stayed in track. As we were going downhill, I, to this day, have no idea what my guide said, but I know I tried to make an adjustment. With that move, the tips of my skis caught a snow bank, and I pitched forward. All of a sudden, Whap! I hit my head on a tree trunk and went down like a shot. I hadn't had that feeling of sudden full force collision since I'd played high school football. I tried to sit up, but my guide told me not to move. My whole right arm and shoulder tingled, and I thought, 'Oh my, I think I've really hurt something.'

"The group behind us stopped, and they were also concerned that I not move my neck. While it did hurt, the unfamiliar sensations I was experiencing on my right side were what scared me as much as anything. The others tried to keep me warm by covering me with their jackets and sent for assistance. After about fifteen minutes, a ski patrol member showed up and asked me questions to make sure that I was conscious and thinking straight. Not long after that, a skimobile with a body basket on the back arrived; and the paramedics started working to get me on a backboard to brace my neck and head.

"Then they zipped me into the basket with blankets, and we started the journey off the mountain. They weren't going fast, but that ride was bumpy and jarred my already tense muscles. In addition to the physical discomfort was the other kind as the different people we passed started asking what had happened. At the base camp I was checked out by the doctor and given a little oxygen. I guess they were worried that I was in shock."

As soon as he could, my friend's sighted guide called Judy at the lodge.

"I was terrified," I've heard Judy say. "I had no way to know how serious the accident had been. So many thoughts go through your head at a time like that. I got to the hospital as quickly as I could, and I waited there for what seemed like an eternity because John was still being transported. Someone told me that it was an encouraging sign that he was being driven to the hospital in an ambulance. They thought that if he were brought in by helicopter it would have meant his condition was more critical. I held on to that bit of hope.

"People have asked me since if I had been upset that he was skiing in the first place. Truthfully, I never felt that way. When I was the most worried, I couldn't help thinking about the worst possibility. But I knew, even then, that if the worst had happened, that John had been on that beautiful mountain doing something he really loved, feeling the freedom of that experience."

As it turned out, after he was transported from the clinic on the mountain to the hospital and the doctors did an MRI, they decided there wasn't any serious damage. They told him he had certainly given himself a real jolt that had caused inflammation in his neck, but the doctor reassured him that he would heal over time. It was a real relief to know that nothing was broken or cracked.

Judy, after her long wait, was overwhelmed with gratitude; and her next thought was for me. Before she hurried from the lodge, she had locked me into their room. Once she talked with the doctor, she immediately called the lodge and someone from SFL came and took me outside. I certainly appreciate her concern for me, and I'm very grateful that I hadn't known anything about all of the excitement and worry of those few hours. I probably shouldn't admit this, but I'm pretty sure I slept through all of it.

Not long after the accident on the mountain, I heard my master talking with some friends who were concerned that he was okay. He told them, "I wish, as we always do after such things, that I had it all to do over again. But my real concern, after the initial fears had been allayed, was whether I'd be healed in time to go on my next ski trip. Believe it or not, I think hitting that tree made me a better, safer, and faster cross country skier."

Yes, it was dangerous, and it was scary for him and Judy; fortunately he didn't injure anything too seriously or permanently. But I believe that he did learn a lot from that accident. He learned about trusting at a level that's appropriate, and he learned about staying within himself when that's the best thing to do. I think I should mention that whenever he tells this story he is very clear about one thing: he doesn't blame his sighted guide for what happened on that trail. He takes the responsibility himself for not making the necessary adjustments because he knew that his guide wasn't as experienced as some others that he's worked with. But he hadn't adjusted to that; he hadn't accommodated his expectations to the circumstances.

Looking back, my friend says that he had continued to plow forward looking to increase his speed and reduce his time instead of telling himself that those goals were not really what the sport is about for him. He knows now that it's about two people working together, adjusting to each other's abilities, while skiing safely to the finish line. This need for accommodating to the circumstances is the same as it has been while working with each of his Seeing Eye dogs. Each one of us has been different with a distinct pace and level of strength and even our own personalities; and he has learned to work within each of his dog's abilities. This is not too different from working with sighted guides in skiing who also have unique personalities and levels of experience.

Even though the skiing hadn't been exactly what my master had anticipated, it was another real learning year at Ski for Light; not only was he a participant, but he also did the announcements at breakfast and dinner. With lots of people wanting all sorts of things publicized, he tried to keep a flow to the announcements each day; it was his job to make sure that everyone had the information as correctly as possible for the day's events. With so many people going to him with requests for announcements, he had to juggle what was appropriate to announce and when. But, of course, everyone thought his was the most important announcement. By using some technology, in this case his Voice Mate, he worked hard to keep all the different people happy with the schedule and the announcements as the week progressed. Being taken from the mountain on a litter and then to the hospital in an ambulance after he had that collision with a tree was also a pretty dramatic learning experience.

One of the things that USA Ski for Light does each year is choose two of the group's skiers and two sighted guides to go to

Norway to an event called the Ridderren; this is where cross-country handicapped skiing began forty-five years ago. It's a real honor to be chosen by SFL to represent the United States in Norway. My buddy was both surprised and elated to be one of those individuals. Soon after he was mostly recovered from his encounter with that tree, he embarked on this trip to Europe without Judy and without me, using only his cane and whatever assistance he could gain from the airline companies and hotels to negotiate his journey.

When he returned from Norway, he was really on a high. "What an experience," he said, "to be able to go to a country where cross-country skiing is their national sport, to be able to participate with four hundred and fifty blind and handicapped skiers from eleven different countries around the world, and to compete in three different events, and at the end of the week do a twenty kilometer race."

He was also enthusiastic about the guide that he had been paired with on this adventure; they had worked on my master's skiing techniques and improved both his style and speed by the end of the week. He was so elated that he had improved his time in the ten kilometer run by over twenty minutes, and then he skied even faster for the twenty kilometer race at the end of the week. If you ask me, that was pretty impressive for someone who had never been on skis until a few short years before.

Chapter Eighteen

'My grace is sufficient for you, for my power is made perfect in weakness.' II Corinthians 12:9

For the first three years that I lived with my master, we went to his job almost every day. I liked going with him. We would walk there in the morning; and I enjoyed that chance to stretch my legs because there were days, when we stayed in his office or were at meetings, that I needed to lie quietly under the table a lot of the time. It was a pleasant walk, and we often passed people who said hello to us or stopped to chat for a minute. It seemed as if everyone knew him, and they soon recognized the two of us as a team. My friend had an important job in our town, and he did things all the time that would help people and solve problems for them. He was so good at what he did, it made me feel proud to be part of his work.

I think the best days then were when we went out to the different offices for my master's business. Yes, they were my favorite times because people always said hello to me and made me feel welcome. Some days were pretty long though, and I was always glad when it was time for us to follow the same route to go back home. I got to know every inch of those streets between home and work so well, it took no effort at all to lead the way.

Then my buddy retired from his job. Now you might think that meant that I retired, too; but I have to tell you I don't feel that way at all. Although our days are different now, I continue to help my master get to all the many places he needs to be; and we still have our routine of walking around town. I've gotten to know all of it now that we're living right in the center. My master and Judy moved here a couple of years ago, actually before he stopped working. It's a pretty old brick house with a white front porch and lots of colorful flowers in the front yard during the warm months. The house is so old that it once belonged to my master's grandparents, and it wasn't new even then. When we first came to live here, I missed our other home a little. But once I got to know all the many rooms, I decided that this house, especially with its family history, is even better. I particularly like our wonderful yard outback where Banner and I can play.

Sometimes, depending on his plans for the day and the weather, the two of us take long walks down in the park that's close to our house. I like getting out for those adventures, especially on nice days. It's always fun when we get to see the geese and the other wildlife that we pass along our way, especially those cute hopping bunnies.

Now that I really know it, I've decided that this is a great little town, and it's filled with a lot of good people. It's also a wonderful place to appreciate all of God's creation. You don't have to go out of town to appreciate this beauty; as I said, you can go into the nearby parks in both the borough and in the townships that surround it. We're very lucky to live here with all of the grass and the trees that make quiet cool places to be in the summer; because we're situated in a valley with a stream that flows through it, we're also somewhat protected from the worst of our Northern weather.

Usually our winters aren't too difficult, but we do get some days of ice and snow. When we get more than a couple of inches, the town workers drive plows along our streets to clear them. I remember a couple of storms when we got more than just a little snow, and all of the intersections were piled high with icy white boulders. Our normal walks around town became a little confusing to me, and I wasn't quite sure which way to lead. I tried going over what seemed like a small mountain; but that turned out to not be a good idea, and we ended up having to walk in the street.

Ice storms, which sometimes occur here in the middle of the night, can be pretty interesting as well. I've heard my partner talk about the morning when we went outside and found that ice had glazed all of our streets and sidewalks. As he remembers it, I just kept on going, digging in with my claws while he held on and glided along behind me. I remember that day, too. I was surprised when the surfaces under my feet seemed to have changed overnight. But I wasn't too concerned, I just grabbed hold of that ice; it was a little more effort to walk than usual, but we had places to go.

All in all, no matter what the weather, it's fun to be able to walk with my friend and help shed a little light and fresh air into his life. I think, from what I've heard him say, that my walks with him help him, too, in his walk with his Lord.

I guess you know by now that the two of us are very close; and because of that, I can tell what he's thinking most of the time. Recently, on one of our morning walks, he decided to take a different route. Usually on these early jaunts all the shops are still closed so we leave our house, and go to the left, pass our church, cross the town streets where most people are still sleeping in their houses, and then go down the playground hill to the walking path. But the last couple of mornings, when we got to what he calls Race Street where he lived as a boy, we made a left and paused for a minute or two before we walked down that street and crossed a few more before turning back toward home.

There was something about this route that felt a little different and seemed to make my buddy smile. I know that walks like this are a good way for him to put his thoughts together; and I wasn't sure I had figured out what he might be thinking until later that morning when we went to the café, and he was having one of those long conversations with his friend Chuck. They greeted each other with smiles and slaps on the back and then got into a conversation which I think shows how talking and looking back over fond memories can be important for people.

First Chuck talked for quite awhile about how things were going in his life and what he was feeling, and my master listened quietly.

They sat together sipping their coffee in silence for a few moments; and then Chuck said, "So how about you? You seem a little subdued this morning. What's been going on for you?"

"Since my retirement, like you, I keep thinking about my life. I guess for the first time in years, I've had time to think beyond the business of each day. Part of it has been about going from the light of the sighted world and then fading slowly over the years into darkness. Now that I'm working on trying to put all of that together in my relationships and my spiritual relationship with my Lord, I find myself drawn back to where I spent so much of my childhood, the house where I lived until I was a junior in high school.

"It sits at the corner of Third and Race Streets. When I was a kid, there was a side yard with a hedgerow that separated the front from the back where I played in the trees and weeded the garden. When I was walking down there, I thought about those times and the lot and barn where I once played and had so many adventures as a boy. It all made me smile as I thought back over all of those good memories.

"But I know things have changed. The house we lived in is still there, but the barn has long since been torn down and replaced with a small shed. The lot, the hedgerow, the gardens, and the trees have all been replaced by a new family's house. I guess these changes make me feel a little nostalgic for the way things once were and the happiness of being a child. I'm pleased for the people who are living there, but progress is always a mixed blessing.

"I went on this new route with Patton because it's also the street that I walked back and forth on when I went to and from elementary school. It's interesting that this morning as we reached the location of our old home, I heard whippoorwills singing in the pine trees across the street where there was once a brickyard; and that sound took me back. But that brickyard, too, is gone; the land is now filled in with houses where it once stood.

"That walk really did make me reminisce, and for some odd reason it made me think about my self-confidence. I was pretty shy when I was a kid. Growing fast, with my size fourteen shoes by the time I was fourteen, and trying to compete in sports, with what I came to know as a handicap with my vision, made me feel awkward and gangly. I never did consider myself a very handsome guy. I always thought my ears were too big, and the list goes on."

Chuck laughed a little at that, "It's funny how much those things mean when we're kids."

"That's true," my master answered with a smile. "It took success in my career to build my confidence; actually being a Marine helped, too, as did my involvements here in the community. In all of those things, I was forced to meet people. Eventually I was able to learn to speak in front of a group although that still takes a lot of effort. Now I just imagine I'm making eye contact with everyone in the room, and I try to have that come through in my voice. But it proves if I can do it anyone can."

"I know what you mean," Chuck answered. "Public speaking is hard for me, too. I think it's great that you kept your confidence throughout the time you were losing your vision."

"There's no question though that it did cause me problems along the way. The hardest thing was becoming increasing dependent on others. People tell me they wouldn't want to lose their sight; and, of course I agree with them. But, you know, it's part of who I am. I've tried to just let it be part of me; having the gift of faith has always allowed me to accept who I am, as I am.

"At the same time, as my vision faded into absolute darkness, it barricaded me from so many things that I like to do. You and I have talked about that before. The loss of sight also robbed me of the ability to see my wife; and I've never seen my children as adults, and I have no image of my grandchildren. Because of these changes sometimes a painful loneliness sets in. No, not all of the time, but often. In those tough moments, I find myself going to God. But I've tried to think about this loneliness and why it exists; is it simply self-pity? And am I allowed to be lonely and feel a little pitiful at times?"

"Of course you're allowed to feel that way," Chuck answered. "But at the same time, as I'm sure you know, there's nothing to be gained by giving in to those feelings. You have to go past them. Believe me, I have to remind myself of that, too."

"Yes, I completely agree, and I do tell myself to get over it. Stop having that pity party for yourself. And get on with it, like you said. For the most part, I've always been able to do that at least as it relates to my blindness. But there's no question that it has sometimes left me with that feeling of being alone. Having a Seeing Eye dog has helped quite a bit. I'm proud of Patton and how we can walk down the street together, and I can usually parlay that feeling into positive energies. But then something will happen, something will go wrong with some part of my life and then, once again, I suddenly feel alone. Yes, pity, I guess it is. Is there a place for self-pity? Do sighted people go through these same feelings?"

"I don't think there's any question about that," Chuck acknowledged. "Even those of us who have no physical problems at all can have a lot of self-pity. I'm pretty convinced that everyone has times of loneliness and, yes, even feeling sorry for yourself. But it seems to me that even though it's true for everybody, when someone is made to feel different it must be worse. As much as we all want to be thought of as special in some ways, I think most people want to feel the same in even more ways."

"I've thought about that," my master said. "Does being blind make me less of a person? I guess some could think of it that way without realizing it. It has all been a lesson for me; and it has helped me in my relationship with God, not that that my relationship with Him is perfect though I wish it were. I would like to go back before the fall of Eden and get up and walk in the morning dew and coolness with God. "

With a little smile, he went on, "One of the advantages in not being able to see, though, is that all of the people I've known for a long time have stayed young in my mind, including you. All of you are just as handsome or beautiful as you were in those great years when we were in our twenties and thirties."

"Now I like that," said Chuck, "although I think you'd be a little surprised by how we look now. But I do like the idea that you see me that way."

"Seriously, I think it's been a good reminder for me that beauty is what's inside a person. I've learned the absolute importance of my true friends, not because of how they look, but for what they really are without any of that as a distraction. The light of what I feel for my family and friends is in my heart. Knowing who is absolutely real with me has been a good thing that's come out of my experiences, and without a doubt all of it has strengthened my faith."

The two men moved on to other things in their conversation, but I was still thinking about my friend and his faith. And that brought me to a question that has sometimes bothered me: If God is so great, why hasn't he allowed my master to regain his sight? I mean here I am, just a dog, and I think about that question; and it makes me wonder. I've heard him reading and sharing out loud the story of men in the Bible who were blind and Jesus restored their sight. Why hasn't that happened for him?

If I were to have a conversation with my buddy, if that were possible like it is with his human friends, I think that would be one of the first questions I would ask him: How is it that you maintain your firm belief in God when he would allow all the things that are so awful in the world to happen, and to you specifically, because you became blind?

I've watched and listened to him, and I think his response would probably sound like this: "First of all, Patton, I want you to think about the fact that if I had not gone blind, I never would have had you, Trevor, or Olive in my life. And my family and friends would never have had the great opportunity to meet and interact with you guys. To me, my dear friend, that's part of God's answer.

"But let's go beyond that because I think that God has allowed me this physical darkness, so that I would have an opportunity to give glory unto God. There is the story in The Scriptures about Jesus and His Disciples, and they came across a blind man sitting by the pool. The Disciples challenged Jesus and asked, 'Why is this man blind? Did his parents sin, did he sin, did his grandparents sin?' And Jesus said, 'No, there is no one to blame, no one who did a particular wrong. This man is blind so that God might be glorified.' Then He made some mud and placed it on the eyes of the man and told him to go wash in the pool. The blind man washed in the pool, and he could see.

"Again, you might say, okay fine, why doesn't God heal you? Well, in my case, God has chosen to use another part of His creation, that would be you, The General, to be my eyes. Is God glorified in this process? Certainly, for it is your purpose, your devotion to me, to show how this love can be translated into a relationship that is dependent, one upon the other, to lead a better life.

"I want you to know, Patton, that doesn't mean that I haven't had bad feelings about having lost my sight; and of course I would dearly love to be able to see my grandchildren, but the fact is that won't happen in this world. So I compensate for it; and I open, as much as I can, my heart and my mind to the light of God's Holy Spirit. I begin each day with my thoughts toward God the Father and allowing the Holy Spirit to enter into my heart.

"What has happened ever since my sight was beginning to fade has been that I was presented with opportunities for glimmers of light, and they come from all different places. Let me give you the example of my children. As they became drivers just when I could no longer drive, that gave me the opportunity for those closest to me to give back by their helping and sharing. And I have met people that I would otherwise have never met if it hadn't been that I would go blind. But it doesn't stop there, Patton. Look at all you give to me and all of the people whom I've gotten to know because I'm with you.

"Think of all of the people who make up the blind community and their families that I have gotten to know through The Seeing Eye, Ski for Light, and in our other travels. We have the opportunity for this sharing in person, and by telephone and email. Think of all the things that we share from what we've learned whether it's in technology or recreational activities or trading experiences and thoughts that are unique to us.

"You know that when I've been at my darkest times, Judy was there for me, my children were there for me, as were my friends, especially those we know through our church. They never faltered. They offered their encouragement and uplifted me.

"But I, too, have had the same question about God and my sight, perhaps not with anger, but with a desperate request to Him. As a matter of fact, one night I was watching a show on television that featured a faith healer. And he was calling people to the front and healing them. People in wheelchairs were getting up and walking. People with all kinds of diseases and problems went forward, and he would lay hands on them. And he said, 'For those of you out there who have problems in your health or spirit, place your hands upon the television. And if your faith is strong enough, you too will be healed.'

"Now I have to tell you, Patton, that I'm kind of a skeptic. I've never gotten very excited about faith healers. But there I was by myself, late at night, standing in front of the television with my hands flat against the screen and my head bowed; and I prayed, 'If it is Your will, then I ask You to restore my sight. But Lord, the most important part is that I may be used to present Your good news of eternal life; and if restoring my sight will do that, I pray You will do that. But if You don't feel that my having sight brings me to a place where I would be of best use to You, then help me to accept Your will in my life.'

"And, of course, Patton, nothing changed with my vision. Would I accept His healing touch and the restoration of my sight? In a heartbeat. But what is most important is that I am open to His indwelling spirit to use me just as I am. We don't know what tomorrow will bring. It's ours to simply live every hour and day striving to help others."

I really believe that's what he would tell me. From my point of view, I think it's very impressive that blind people, including my dear friend, always go forward with their lives. In spite of what they must sometimes feel about being alone and isolated, perhaps even feeling rejected or shunned, they keep going. Actually, I believe that's true for all people with handicaps or other differences who are made to feel isolated for all kinds of reasons.

As a dog, I certainly can't stand to be alone, and I don't like feeling isolated. Sometimes when I'm in my crate, I wonder: Is he rejecting me? I don't think so, but sometimes, you can feel that way. I don't know about humans for sure but from what I've seen with them, when they're genuine with their love, it can lead to full trust. All kinds of differences can evaporate within that trust. But something a person has to guard against is the depths of darkness and feeling they are not able to catch up to where others are or to be able to go as fast as they can. Perhaps when it happens for them, the darkness can become dangerously consuming. The good news is that the light that comes from many places gives all people a lift. For handicapped people are people, too, with the same feelings of success or sense of rejection. This is true for everyone no matter how different others or circumstances might make her or him feel.

Even in the times when my master is feeling a little nostalgic, each day we get up and begin our day together. This very morning, a beautiful July day with the sun just coming up through the trees, we again walked along the stream. In places we could hear it as it babbled across the stones. In my head, I was kind of singing a song along with the morning birds who seemed to be saying, "It's time to get up, it's time to start the day." As we walked along, I heard my good buddy start humming one of his favorite hymns; I knew then that we were together in feeling the promise of this new day.

Chapter Nineteen

Love is patient, love is kind. It does not envy, it does not boast, it is not proud.   I Corinthians 13:4

Once he was actively involved in his newfound love of cross-country skiing, my master was presented with the chance to take on another challenge. This time it was fishing. Being so involved in sports as a boy, especially spring and summer baseball, he had never had too much experience with fishing. Just as he was a little surprised to find himself skiing after he had lost his vision, at first he wasn't too sure about this new idea. But once again he thought he'd just give it a try and see how things went. Not being a person who does much of anything halfway, he didn't just mosey down to the stream that meanders through our town and drop in a line. No, not him; he decided to take up an offer to join a group of his friends and venture to a remote reservoir in Canada, far beyond anything that we think of as civilization.

Because of the different logistics, I couldn't go with him. I'll admit to you that during the times he goes away without me, I get quite a bad case of separation anxiety. I know I shouldn't, but the fact is I do. He almost never leaves me behind, and I guess I've gotten a little better about it over time. But I like to be able to see him, even if he's not talking to me. I just like being there, wherever he is; and not having me to guide him on this trip would also mean that he would need to rely, at least a little, on the eyes of his fishing companions.

At the beginning there was a great deal of discussion about the wisdom of my friend's joining the group for this fishing expedition. Not being able to drive the boats, as well as having had no prior fishing experience, created a great deal of conversation as to how he would handle the challenges and fare as a fisherman. Because of the potential problems involved, at moments even he wondered if this offer was given out of friendship or if it was actually some kind of scientific experiment.   The truth is that there were concerns from almost all quarters; even his family members were divided on the decision. Their realistic apprehensions were mostly focused on issues of safety. I understand different people's fears for him, and sometimes I feel that way, too. Yet at the same time, I really do know that it's important for him to stay active and keep on trying new things. He would probably be pretty safe all the time if he just sat around in our home, but that would never work with his personality.

His friend who was organizing the trip, the man known in the group as The Walleye Professor, believed all along that his pal could fish just as well as a sighted person and that there was no reason for worry. He's an accomplished fisherman with many years of experience in sporting excursions behind his opinion; so, in the end, his judgment helped seal the decision.

The Walleye Professor is just one of the cast of characters that make up this group of men, and they all have original names that they've given each other. First you have to understand that because my friend was the only one who was going on this expedition for the first time, he was initially referred to as The Rookie. Once that name had lost some of its meaning, he was relabeled L.J., which stands for Little John. Now in order to fully appreciate that second nickname, you need to know that my master is, at six foot three inches, the tallest of the four that went. He gladly accepted both of these labels as part of that camaraderie and needling that goes on among the guys, especially this particular group of guys. The other three were The Walleye Professor, who I mentioned is the leader of the group; Tommie One Keeper, who earned his name through an event from a past fishing trip; and J.C., which are actually the correct initials for his name. I guess you can tell from these nicknames that guys, at least these guys, just can't call each other by their given names.

Once it was all decided and The Walleye Professor had taken care of all the many details that such an expedition requires, this foursome took off for Canada very early one morning in the middle of June. From their homes, it is an eleven-hour drive to upper Quebec. Their destination was a town called Mont-Laurier where they were to stay overnight, so they'd be ready for the final leg of their journey in the morning. Carrying a large quantity of food and fishing gear, the four split up into two rooms. They took the most important items in with them to keep in the refrigerator, and that, of course, included the most important one of all, the bait.

As they got settled in for the night, L.J., The Rookie, was suddenly more than a little bit nervous about the whole trip; and he couldn't help thinking about the fact that the next day would be the start of an experience that was totally new for him. They would be going to the outfitters and getting on pontoon planes to fly one hour farther north; then they were to land on the water at a place called the Gouin Reservoir. They were to stay there, completely disconnected from all civilization, for a week with nothing to do but to tell bad stories, play cards, and fish. The fact that he was now committed was suddenly feeling more than a little daunting.

The next morning after resting up, they got ready to check out of the motel and continue their journey.

As they were leaving their room, J.C. said to L.J., "Well, let's go. It's time to get headed north."

L.J. asked him, "Are you sure we have everything?"

"I checked, and we're ready to go."

"Why don't we stop and think a minute," L.J. suggested. "Because there's one item that we really need to take along. "

At that point, it hit J.C. that the all-important worms were still in the fridge. Laughing heartily at each other, they went out to the car, at which point J.C. told The Professor and Tommie One Keeper, "The Rookie has just earned his keep: he remembered the bait."

After driving a little bit north to the outfitters and getting all the gear as well as themselves weighed in, the four embarked upon the pontoon plane and got set for at least an hour of no communication; it's impossible to hear each other or even talk over the roar of the plane's engine. For my friend, that flight was a strange and disconnected experience. He couldn't see the scenery the others were enjoying or see their expressions, which left him feeling totally isolated within the vibrations of the plane and all of its noise.

Finally they landed safely on the water, and that sensation must have been a great relief to my master. Arriving at the cabin site just shortly after lunch, the four got themselves semi organized, grabbed their fishing gear, and set off for the water. They divided into pairs so there would be two men to each boat. Once they got going, they headed out into the reservoir to catch their meal for the evening. For that is the Walleye Professor's rule: the meal for Saturday night, the first night, is whatever they were able to catch. Later, as the day was closing and after catching enough fish for supper, the four returned to the cabin for their first walleye meal at the Goin Reservoir.

Once they were settled in, the week was filled with lots of fun, laughter, and needling, those very things that guys always do together. After all the concerns that preceded the trip, you may wonder how the rookie fared as a fisherman. I guess you'd have to say he had a slow start. Upon donning his brand new fishing clothing, including a pair of calf high boots to keep his feet dry, he appeared at the doorway ready to go out on that Saturday's first fishing expedition.

As he stood there, Tommie One Keeper looked him over and asked, "So Rookie, how do those boots feel?"

L.J. responded, "Well, I guess they feel a little tight. But they're new. They'll probably loosen up a little once I've worn them awhile."

Tommie One Keeper was silent for a moment, and then he said, "I bet they'd feel better even sooner if they were on the right feet."

The Rookie had proven how much he really was a first timer by putting his unfamiliar boots on wrong; it was no wonder that they felt tight. He would, of course, do other things during the week to demonstrate that he was, indeed, a rookie. Having never fished before and experiencing the Gouin Reservoir for the first time were challenges enough; being a blind man added some complications. But he often says that the care, understanding, and friendship displayed by the other three and by the caretaker of the campsites made a great difference.

Every day they had to get from the cabin to the dock and then into the boat. The caretaker, a fellow named Josie who is a French Canadian, would kneel down and help L.J. steady himself on the dock while he held the boat for him to get in safely. When they returned to the dock after fishing, Josie was always right there to ensure that my master was able to get back on dry land. From what I've heard the guys say, when you first meet him you might think that Josie is a little gruff; but once you're around him awhile you get a very different idea of what he's like.

In addition to the fun of the fishing was the good-natured companionship that took place at meal times. Each person had his jobs, and everybody pitched in to make sure that all of them were fed with plenty of food. Of course walleye was on the menu many times, cooked in a variety of ways, for The Walleye Professor has created several dishes over the years that are very tasty. In the evenings, the four took turns espousing on various topics of general interest, and some of it included poking fun at each other's expertise and finesse as a fisherman. Everyone had his own special techniques and favorite lures. The careful and sometimes debated noting of each day's catch statistics reinforced the sense of competition.

Then there was the infamous Hearts card game. As part of the tradition of going to the Gouin Reservoir, for The Walleye Professor and particularly Tommie One Keeper, there is always a Hearts tournament. This trip was going to be a little different because my master took along two decks of cards that are Braille embossed in the corners. They embarked on teaching L.J. how to play the game while he showed them how to play the tournament with the Braille cards.

I've heard it said that my master was leading in the tournament after two hands.

At that point, one of his sighted friends whose name we won't say except to mention it wasn't J.C. or The Walleye Professor, started complaining a little, "Okay now that we've played a couple of hands in the dark, I think it's time we turned on the lights. Let's give the sighted guys a chance to win, too."

My buddy reluctantly agreed to the new rules, and Tommie One Keeper proceeded to win the Hearts tournament. There seems to be some continuing debate about the fairness of having the lights on or off under the circumstances, but then they tell their story their way.

Oh, and then there was the fishing. Well, they caught quite a few fish, mostly walleye but there were also pike. The Walleye Professor and Tommie One Keeper caught over a hundred each; J.C. caught somewhere in the range of sixty fish; and interestingly, going into the last day on the Gouin, The Rookie had caught twenty-two. But it was that last day when my master really did shine. After making a few adjustments to some of his fishing rig and going out for the first time with Tommie One Keeper, my friend caught eighteen fish on that last outing which made him the "high hook" for the day and allowed him to finish the week with forty fish. He tells people he went to the Gouin and caught forty fish. He kind of leaves the story there because those people are pretty impressed that he caught forty fish in one week, even though the complete truth is that he was low man of the four. But, in the way of fishermen, that can be pointed out later if it's absolutely necessary.

After hearing so many stories about this adventure, I've come up with a little theory. It's that though the fishing was the stated reason for the trip, the point of it all is actually friendship. From my time of being around people and watching things pretty closely, I believe that friends don't ask each other what is your strength or what are your weaknesses. They accept each other for who they are and what they are. They reach out to each other to lift them up when they're down or to sing their praises when they're up. Then there is the simple fact of being a friend, and the question about what that is. Everyone has many acquaintances, but what is a friend? To me it means that we have someone we know that we can lean on, someone who doesn't ask what's in it for him or what will it cost him. Friends are those who will help simply because the help is needed; they will listen because their friend needs to talk or talk when someone needs to listen. They don't even need to agree all of the time. Though this group on the trip spent a lot of time kidding and heckling each other, at the base under all the jokes, is their friendship.

Speaking of poking a little fun, my master tells a story that perhaps J.C. wishes wouldn't be told; but for my master it's an important part of his memories of that first trip to the Gouin

Reservoir. One afternoon after The Walleye Professor and Tommie One Keeper had already gone out, my friend and J.C. rested for a while and then they, too, headed out to see what they could catch. It had been raining, so the boat had some water in it. J.C. started bailing at the same time he was driving the boat.

Not realizing what was happening and thinking they were headed in the right direction because of the wake from the motor, he was unintentionally pushing the boat more and more to the right. As J.C. continued to bail and drive, all of a sudden there was a booming thud as the boat stopped with a terrifying jolt. My friend has a strong memory of this incident because he didn't know what had happened or what they had hit; but he knew that they must have hit something after the boat came to an abrupt stop. Having been thrown forward from the force of the collision, he found himself on his knees in the bottom of the boat. He couldn't imagine what was going on around him in the quiet that followed the impact, and he had no idea if J.C. was okay or even if he was still in the boat.

He cried out to him, "Hey J.C.; are you okay?"

When he didn't immediately answer, my master remembers the thoughts that he had for his fishing buddy's well being. As it happens in such situations, he remembers a lot of what went through his head in that flash of time that actually felt much, much longer.

Finally J.C. answered, "Well L.J., it looks as if we've gotten ourselves wedged between two rocks on the shore."

You can imagine the relief my friend felt when he heard that voice and those words; and fortunately, neither one of them was injured at all. The two actually laugh quite a bit now about what happened that day and how the boat came to be landed on the shore in that rather ungainly way. Though he never includes this part in his story, I think it must have been pretty terrifying for him in those first moments until he knew that J.C. was all right. Imagine being in the middle of nowhere, surrounded by blackness, and suddenly being confronted with the thought that you're completely alone. Considering all of the horrifying possibilities, it might be that you were responsible for the survival of your buddy as well as yourself because there was no way to tell where the other two guys might be on that immense reservoir. Happily, the potential terror was soon replaced by laughter.

Since they had both served in the military, they talk about it now as being the assault on the beaches of the Gouin Reservoir; and they plan, for their next trip, that the storming of the beaches will be better planned and a little more strategically placed. When I hear this story, what I mostly hear is that feeling of friendship, that sense of having a buddy, and wondering, is he okay? Had he passed out, was he thrown from the boat, or other equally frightening possibilities? Of course, none of those things happened, and now they tease about it as guys do.

I know it might sound a little exaggerated, but my master talks about this incident and then adds, "It's the kind of friendship that you see in foxholes and in bunkmates in the Marines, and in landing parties at Normandy Beach."

Is this overly dramatic? Perhaps it is, but it gives you a sense of how he feels about the value of friends like J.C., The Walleye Professor, and Tommie One Keeper.

I really have to wonder about what kind of trust it must take for a man to travel to the north of Quebec to go fishing in a remote area where he has never been and has no way to envision. Maybe that speaks to what real friendship is about, for it is this trust that my master has for his fishing partners. I know that he realizes that they may well have sacrificed some of their own good fun and fishing to help him to learn, but he also knows that they did it only out of a desire to do it. The good news is that they've invited him back to go fishing again. That says something about them, and I would like to think it says something about my master as well.

Chapter Twenty

Your word is a lamp to my feet, and a light for my path.
Psalm 119:105

While my friend and I are out on our walks, there are several stores in town where we go to buy various items that are needed at the house. I've built a relationship with many of the people in these shops; I especially love to go into the store called The Deli where they give me biscuits. I think going to that shop and the local bank branch are my favorites because at both places the people who work there make a big fuss over me. Who wouldn't want to go back over and over again? There are restaurants in our little town that we also visit from time to time in the evenings for dinner. Then, of course, there's our neighborhood café where we spend so many good times with people and where my master has so many interesting conversations.

Just the other morning when we stopped in to the café, a bunch of guys from The Group were there. As it happened that day, all of them were retired; and eventually their new circumstances became the subject of their conversation.

One of the men, Joe, who uncharacteristically seemed a little down, said to the others, "Do you ever get the feeling the journey might be finished?"

Another man named Larry answered immediately, "Oh, I don't feel that way at all. Not one bit. We are just at a place where things have changed pretty abruptly. Sometimes changes feel like endings when they're really beginnings. We are retired, and I say we've earned it."

At that they all raised their coffee mugs and said, "Hear, hear!"

My master then said, "I'm not even sure that I ever thought much about retirement or what life would be like when I stopped working. But I certainly hope my journey, which has taken so many twists and turns, isn't over."

"Do you mean to say you never thought about being retired?" Larry asked with surprise. "I think I looked forward to it every day for the last ten years I worked. "

"It's just that after being in business for forty years, I am now away from that fast pace and all the social aspects that went with it. It's taking some getting used to," my friend answered.

The man named Joe who had begun this conversation started to laugh and added, "It's funny I said what I did because I'm one of those people who feel so busy all the time that I'm not sure how I ever found time to work."

"You've got a point there," my master answered. "I guess for me it's still very important to continue to be able to help others. For in the end that's what I think it's all about. Now I'm focusing on volunteer work."

"Maybe we've spent enough years taking care of other people all the time," suggested Larry. "And don't forget that now we have the chance for all the travel and vacations we always thought we'd do and never made the time for."

"That's a funny thing that I'm learning to get used to, too. Those trips before seemed a lot more meaningful when I was so involved in my work. Now that I'm not active in that way, I'm not exactly sure what the meaning of vacation actually is."

"Now that's a pity," Joe said with pretend sympathy. "Those skiing and fishing trips you go on must be such a bother now."

With that everyone did laugh, including my friend. Then they went on to talk about the trips and vacations they had taken or were planning. By the time they had their last round of coffee, they had ended up agreeing that retirement, while requiring some changes in their point of view, really had a whole lot of good things going for it.

Later that day, from what he was saying to me, I could tell that this conversation was still on my friend's mind. That he does sometimes talk to me might sound a little unusual; but I think he does it to clear his mind, and I was happy to listen when he said,

"But this I do know: the fears that I felt when I was going to bed in the attic have been replaced by the fears of each new adventure.

And being retired is definitely another adventure for me. I know that at the very heart of the matter is the ability to trust in God to always be present to help overcome how I fear each new journey. But then, do I want to completely stop those feelings? There's a part of me that knows that a little apprehension helps motivate me to prepare. And maybe that's not all bad."

I was glad my buddy came to that good conclusion, and he seemed much more cheerful after he had thought it through. Actually, it seemed to me that he had done a lot of thinking lately; and he was putting the things that had been troubling him into a much happier perspective. It made me feel good that he was so much more like his usual self. I couldn't help thinking that sometimes it's important for people to talk about the things that are on their minds.

As for me though, I was still feeling pretty happy about our time at the café that day. Everybody there knows me. Some of them give me little pats on the head, and usually I'm offered a bowl of water. It's great going there with all those smells on the floor; you know what that's like in a restaurant where bits and pieces happen to fall. I don't mind helping to clean the place up a little sometimes. Don't tell my master, but who knows what I might find on the floor? Sometimes it might be a French fry; sometimes it's a bit of egg or a home fry. You never can tell what a day will bring your way, and this morning it was a little piece of toast with butter and jam on it.

Then there are those times that we go places outside of town; and, instead of walking, we get a ride from a friend or Judy drives our family car. I just love hopping in and going along, and I'm always curious to see the sights and try to figure out where we're headed. Sometimes our trips are fairly short, and then there are other times we go for longer rides for vacations or special visits. On those longer trips, I relax and enjoy the ride. It's nice to know that no matter where we might be headed, I'm always welcome, even in those places where dogs are usually not allowed to go. Fortunately, because we guide dogs are so well trained and have an important job to do, there are laws that insure that we can go everywhere that people do.

Thinking about traveling with my friend reminds me of something that happened a couple of weeks ago. I guess you can tell by now that not too much ever bothers me; and I think this little story shows that about me. My master was packing a suitcase for one of his trips. I was staying near him in case he needed me, but after awhile I decided the job he was doing might take a little while. What seemed like the best thing to do was to stay clear of their path as he and Judy moved around selecting and organizing his clothes and things. I decided that a good place to stay out of the way was on the floor of the closet, and I curled up in there for a little rest to wait and see what was next. Having just come in from a run in the backyard, I was feeling a little sleepy.

I guess I must have dozed off and didn't even realize they had finished what they were doing and closed the closet door. The next thing I knew, I heard Banner barking from the other side of the door. It sounded as if she was very concerned about something; and when Judy came to check to see what was going on, we both discovered that Banner had been worried about me. That sweet girl dog was a good friend to be concerned, and I gave her a little nudge when I went out to thank her and to let her know that I had been fine all along and had enjoyed my nap.

That closet door story makes me think of the day that David came over to help his dad with a little job. We have an upstairs porch like a lot of the older houses in our neighborhood. Because there aren't any steps on the outside, the only way to get out there is through a door near the upstairs laundry room. David and his dad had gone out to the porch, leaving the door ajar. I had been in another room and decided I'd like to see what the two of them were up to. When I realized that they were out there on the porch, I pushed the door with my nose to open it wider so I could go be with them.

But instead of opening the door, my little nudge actually pushed it shut. I had no idea that the latch had been set to lock when the door closed. When that happened, I was feeling pretty disappointed that I couldn't be outside, too. It was about the same time that they realized what had I had done. There they were, stuck outside on the second floor with no way to get in and no way to get down. Or that's what they thought at first, and I could tell they thought it was pretty comical. Judy wasn't at home just then, and they knew she planned to be out for a couple of hours. As they considered how to escape from that second floor perch, David checked a nearby window to see if it was also locked. Fortunately, he was able to get into the house that way. I wasn't sure what he meant when he came in and called me a little goof; but he gave me a pat on the head and smiled, so I knew that everything was fine.

Thinking about these stories reminds me that our family has little adventures all the time that make us feel good; but my favorite days now are the ones when we get the chance to spend time with my friend's three grandchildren, two boys and a little girl. I think they're his best days, too. Sometimes the kids visit us at our house, or we go to see them at theirs. I think it's wonderful for the whole family that these children live in the same town as where my master and his own kids grew up and where everyone agrees that it is an ideal place to raise a family. Because we all live close to each other, we also go to almost all of the children's activities.

Just like both of their parents, the boys are excellent athletes; and we try to get to all of their games. And that precious girl is so good at everything she does that I bet we'll soon be going to her activities, too. Sometimes we go to high school baseball games because their dad is the coach and their uncle David works with him; actually it's the same team that my buddy pitched for when he was in school. All of these events are fun, even though I'm not all that crazy about sitting in bleachers. That's a bit awkward for me to maneuver.

Watching those kids is just amazing; I think they are very special people. I know that my master feels the same way about them. We were at a friend's house yesterday, and this is what he had to say when he was asked about them, "They are twelve, nine and six, now. It's wonderful to watch one of your children taking on the role of mom, but it's even more exciting to be Nanny and Pop Pop. Nanny of course spoils all three of them, and Pop Pop just beams a lot. I'm not sure, but it might be more fun to be a grandparent than it was a parent because we can do all these terrific things with them and leave the other parts more to their mom and dad."

Then he added, "Just as I had the advantage of grandparents in my life as I was growing up, these children now have the same thing. I think that I benefited greatly from having that generation actually living with us. I'd like to think that Judy and I and the kids' grandparents on their father's side can have influence in a similar positive way, reaching across the generations to our grandchildren. Now that we're retired we can offer a lot of assistance with running the children around, whether it is to school events or to their Little League activities. And it's especially nice to be living close enough to our grandchildren to participate in their growth and their learning. I am hopeful that God will allow us to do that for a number of years and that we can see another generation mature, find their talents, and give back as we have watched our own children do."

Seeing my master and his wife with their grandchildren is one more reminder to me of how important love is to people. I really think it's the most significant thing in their lives. How does one explain the power of love when it takes on so many different forms and is shown in so many ways? There is the love between a husband and wife, the love for their children and their grandchildren, the love for a friend, and, of course, the love for God. And there's even the love for your Seeing Eye dog, and the dog's for its master. Love exists in so very many ways, and yet each has elements that are the same. I've heard my friend talk about the fact that in languages other than his there are words to describe all these different kinds of love. That seems like a good idea to me, but then I'm limited to wagging my tail or rubbing up against someone to show how I feel.

The first time I learned about these different kinds of love happened not long after I arrived here from The Seeing Eye. Judy often goes to bed first; and one night I went upstairs with her to lie at the foot of the bed, which of course I had been trained not to do. But, well you know, the master wasn't there yet, so why not? On this particular night, he eventually came upstairs and his wife appeared to be sleeping. I was still lying where I wasn't supposed to be, but I soon realized he wasn't upset that I was there.

After getting ready for bed, he knelt down, patted my head, and said, "Patton, I love you so much. You're such a good boy."

Then, in the pause and silence that followed, we heard Judy quietly say, "When is the last time you knelt by the bed and stroked my hair, and said, 'I love you so much'?"

My buddy's response was more or less a "Whoops!"

But then, of course, they laughed together. For they understand, as I was to learn, that love exists and enriches our lives in many different ways. That little incident was a good reminder, too, for my master. Sometimes it's easy to forget to show the love and appreciation we feel for those who are closest to us.

At our church, there is often a lot of talk about love. My favorite part of the Bible even says what I just mentioned: that love is the most important thing there is. I always listen especially closely when this passage is discussed. It's there that we learn about love in the broadest sense. Through these verses we can have a clear understanding of the kind of love that Jesus teaches us, and it doesn't have anything to do with our own self-interest but has everything to do with reaching out and embracing others. I see this love in all of my friend's relationships. These very personal bonds continue to teach him how to allow light from outside himself enrich his life and give him the strength to reach back. For as it says in the Bible, "And now these three remain: faith, hope and love. But the greatest of these is love."

From all that I've told you, you may think that I'm pretty special when in fact I am, and will always remain, just a dog. Am I trained for a specific purpose? Yes, and I try to do the best job I can. In fact, I like to think that I provide a unique light to my master's life. A stranger watching us might think that means just guiding him wherever he goes, but I believe it's much more than that. I know that I do provide a guidance system for him; but I also provide friendship, love, fun, and, yes, sometimes even therapy. Through all the time I've spent with him, quietly observing and listening, I believe that I've come to understand the journey that has been my friend's life. Though he now lives in darkness, I see that he has always worked to turn that into a positive. From listening to him talk about his relationships with others and with his Master, I've come to believe that this whole thing about light and dark can be complex; and yet in the end, like most things, I believe it is also simple.

So, I don't know about you, but it seems to me it might be time for a big biscuit. That gets my juices flowing. I sit back with that treat and just relax and get ready for a good night's rest. As for my friend, I think his Big Biscuit is already assured, for just like when he forgives me, correction is made and forgiveness is given, and then we both move forward. In a way, you might say that he's been switched. Now we all know when we want to turn a light on we turn the switch; to turn it off, we turn the switch, too. The switch I'm talking about is The Light of the World in the form of God's Son when He switched places with my master. For that matter, Jesus changed places for all people; and with that act of going to the cross and then rising from the dead, He switched on a light for the whole world.

For you see, light does not only come from a light bulb. The overcoming of the little boy's fear of the darkness in the attic never really had anything to do with the light switch. When he dashed across the attic and dove into his bed, it was because of his fears of not knowing. As that child matured and turned into a man, he no longer needed the light from the light bulb to know that he was safe. For as that man continued to grow and journey through this life and found that he would be facing the physical darkness of the lost light of his eyes, he matured and learned how to use the resources within and around him. In time he came to know that it was not with his eyes that he saw but with his mind and heart. In his spiritual life, that ongoing journey of new beginnings, that light exists for him just as it can exist for all people. For it is this light that gets switched on when we come to understand the fullness of God's grace.

There you have it. Just as I am excited to go for walks to guide my master, he is excited to go for walks with his Master and through Him to shine light for others. And like me, at the end of the day he's ready to kick back and have a big biscuit and a little talk with his

Master, and maybe get a little pat on his head from Him. I know that's what I enjoy: to get that big biscuit, a little pat on the head, and to hear, "Atta Boy, Patton."

Acknowledgements

After my retirement from a forty year career with one company, one in which I often sacrificed time from my family, I thought it would be interesting to leave them a record of my journey to this time. Sitting down with my tape recorder and memories, I began to recall the many stories, adventures, valleys crossed, and mountains climbed along the way. As I continued through this process, I decided it would be a fun thing for my grandchildren to have these recollections as told by my Seeing Eye dog. The process blossomed into this book about my journey and the profound connection of complete trust found in my relationships with my Seeing Eye dogs and my relationship with God.

We all relive and recount the past within the framework of our own perspective. Who is to say which memories are right, except where they are recorded or captured by images through modern technology? Even then, we have found that some have altered memories to fit their own purpose. With this in mind, I would beg your indulgence.

Meaning not to forget anyone and fully appreciating everyone who has ever shared my path, I would like to thank some very special people, all of who have helped me and motivated me to continue. First and foremost, Judy, I could have never made it without you. Your belief in me and our purpose in this life have always helped me to keep the right things in focus. I love you! Mom and Dad, who gave me both life and faith, how can I ever thank two of the finest Christians I have ever known. To the family, our children and grandchildren, our brothers and sisters and all their loved ones: you have always inspired and supported me. Pastor Blaik and my friend Chuck, my two prayer partners, you have helped me to have a better understanding of God's Word. Stu and John, thanks for caring and encouraging me. Denny, I have always looked up to you; you are a spiritual inspiration.

There are so many others: former teachers, coaches, Sunday school teachers, and all my friends who never turned away from me and who hugged Judy and me when we needed it. To Pam, my writer, who took the thoughts and memories I dictated and turned them into written form. Thank you to The Seeing Eye, especially the instructors/trainers. And how about those puppy raisers? Many, many thanks to you! Seeing Eye volunteers give so much, which makes it possible for visually impaired people to have the independence with dignity that we can experience by having a guide dog. Thank you!

We cannot leave this page without a special mention of the three Seeing Eye dogs that have guided me along my life's path; a big hug and a really big biscuit for Trevor, Olive, and Patton. Just think how lucky my future guide dogs will be because the three of you have made me a better dog handler... and a dog lover.

And yet, there is always one more to whom I give eternal thanks. His name is Jesus, and He lives and is everything to me. Indeed, He is the light of the world.

John Hollenbach

It has been a true pleasure for me to know John and Judy as close friends since the days when he and I served together on our local school board. The times my husband, who is also named John, and I have spent with them are among our favorite memories. We have always had great respect for their strength as a couple as we've watched John prevail through the challenges of his diminishing vision, and we've thoroughly enjoyed knowing all three of his remarkable Seeing Eye dogs.

On a beautiful fall morning when the four of us were away on a weekend retreat with a group of mutual friends, John approached me with the idea of collaborating on a memoir of what I knew to be his eventful and inspiring life. Having just left my former world as a librarian and teacher of English and considering my profound appreciation for John's life story, I was immediately both enthusiastic and honored by the prospect.

In our first of numerous conversations concerning our project, John told me that he envisioned Patton as his book's narrator. My first thought was that developing his Seeing Eye dog into a credible storyteller would present unique and possibly unconquerable challenges for both of us, but we decided to proceed and see if we could make it work. While John continued to record his thoughts and I transcribed them and worked them into a narrative, it turned out that, as rewarding as it was working with my human counterpart, giving voice to his beloved dog was equally gratifying. When his master and I would meet to discuss our work's progress, I would often sit on the floor with Patton, with his harness removed, to experience his gentle serenity. He is an extraordinary creature: patient, dependable, and unfailingly kind. Portraying his wisdom has been an enormously gratifying adventure.

With thanks and love to my husband, children, and friends, and to John and Judy for the faith and trust they have placed in me to help tell their story.

Pam Cressman

John D. Hollenbach is available for speaking engagements and personal appearances. For more information contact:

John D. Hollenbach
C/O Advantage Books
P.O. Box 160847
Altamonte Springs, Florida 32716

To purchase additional copies of this book or other books published by Advantage Books call our toll free order number at:
1-888-383-3110 (Book Orders Only)

or visit our bookstore website at:
www.advbookstore.com

Longwood, Florida, USA
"we bring dreams to life" ™
www.advbooks.com